top 50
FRAGRANT PLANTS

*and how **NOT** to kill them!*

ANGIE THOMAS

HarperCollins*Publishers*

CONTENTS

INTRODUCTION

Fragrance has the powerful ability to instantly transport you back to a place, person or time. It could be a childhood memory of the scent of freshly mown grass in the backyard, the intoxicating fragrance of frangipanis carried on a gentle breeze during a tropical holiday or your favourite aunt's flowery perfume. Fragrances can also help you feel more positive, induce a sense of calm and reduce stress. Doesn't just the thought of burying your nose in among the delicate petals of a heavenly scented rose make you want to close your eyes and smile dreamily?

The power of fragrance is demonstrated by the worldwide perfume industry reportedly being worth more than US$32 billion. People just love inhaling beautiful scents! Even many household cleaning products, detergents and washing powders are infused with botanical-based fragrances, showing how enamoured we are with scent. With fragrances capable of being so alluring, evocative and entrancing, it's fortunate that gardeners have the magnificent opportunity to grow and enjoy the plants that produce many of these scents. What a treat to be able to step out into a garden, courtyard or balcony, and be surrounded by a collection of your favourite fragrant flowers and foliage. Mother Nature's perfumery!

Of the five senses – sight, hearing, touch, taste and smell – sight is usually ranked as the most important, with taste and smell perceived as being the least valuable senses. However, it is not until a person's sense of smell is adversely affected that its power is recognised. Smell plays an important part in the taste and enjoyment of meals (as well as the detection of spoiled food), and losing the ability to smell (called anosmia) has been shown to affect a person's quality of life, feelings of personal safety and emotional wellbeing. So, smell may have a low ranking, but it's definitely a sense that should be valued and appreciated.

Sight, hearing, touch and taste information is first analysed by the thalamus, a part of the brain sometimes referred to as the 'gatekeeper'. This information is then passed on to the body and other parts of the brain for processing. However, smell is handled differently. Smells are analysed by our olfactory bulbs, which are structures that sit in the front base of the brain above the nasal cavities. The smell information is not processed by the thalamus; instead, the 'messages' are sent directly to parts of the brain that are responsible for memory, emotion and cognition. This could be part of the reason that fragrances elicit such powerful connections with feelings and memories.

CLOCKWISE FROM TOP LEFT: Gardenia; jasmine; roses

Studies with rats have shown that their sense of smell is closely linked to positive and negative brain reactions, which influence their learning and formation of memories. The researchers theorise that this is 'why the sense of smell plays such a unique role in the formation and retrieval of memories'.[1] Further investigation is needed to untangle the science of smell; however, knowledge to date indicates a fascinating link between what we smell and the intricate recesses of our mind.

There is also research that looked at whether a person's sense of smell could be improved and whether it had wider effects, beyond 'just' smell. 'Smell training' trials, in which older adults were given different strong odours to smell over several months, saw promising results, with improvements in not only smell detection but also cognitive tasks.[2] Scientists feel that these benefits could be due to the olfactory (smell) network being 'particularly neuroplastic',[3] meaning that it can improve neural pathways or form new ones. Another German study showed that people could enhance their sense of smell by sniffing intense rose, eucalyptus, lemon and clove scents twice a day for 12 weeks.[4] So, we may have the capacity to improve our sense of smell and also positively influence our cognitive abilities. It's exciting to know that the fragrance of flowers and foliage can be more than just pleasant. It can be brain-changing!

A complete loss or diminishing sense of smell is one of the early signs of neurodegenerative diseases such as Alzheimer's and Parkinson's, as well as being a natural part of ageing. It is also a symptom of COVID-19 infection, with some people experiencing ongoing disturbances in their sense of smell. The United States National Institutes of Health reported that research conducted with dementia patients who had Alzheimer's disease indicated that aromatherapy with lemon balm, lavender and citrus could reduce agitation, improve mood, and have a positive effect on concentration and memory.[5] Incorporating fragrant plants in 'pick and sniff' and sensory gardens in dementia facilities is also showing promise, often helping stimulate memories and senses.

Perfumes were first recorded as being used in ancient civilisations about 5000 years ago, and their popularity continues. Modern-day perfumers are constantly striving for magical combinations of scents to capture the hearts, minds and noses of consumers. Many perfumes are designed with three different 'notes': the top, middle and base. The top note is the first (but not long-lasting) scent that is noticed; citrus is often included in this note. The middle (or heart) note follows; it is usually the most dominant fragrance and is quite persistent. Lavender and rose are often used as middle notes. Finally, the base note is rich and long-lasting, with patchouli and vanilla being common choices.

LEFT: Madagascar jasmine and hyacinth

Some flowers have a blend of these notes, helping to create a complex natural fragrance; rose breeders, for example, will often describe their varieties as having these different levels of fragrance. This can help you choose which rose to include in your garden: you may be drawn to a particular fragrance description, such as a citrus top note with a peachy middle and a patchouli base. However, one of the best ways to choose a fragrant plant is to seek it out while it's in full bloom (or peak foliage) and inhale! Sometimes words are not enough to adequately capture their full aromatic bliss.

Some scents can be quite polarising. For example, many people adore the intense fragrance of jonquils, while others compare the smell to cat urine! So just like food preferences, the fondness for different perfumes is personal. There are also scents that will send some people running for their allergy medication. Floral fragrances are composed of a complex blend of constituents, which can vary between plants and even between varieties of the same plant, and they may push allergy sufferers into unpleasant territory. So, scent-sensitive people will need to work out which plants trigger a reaction and avoid planting those in their gardens. With more than 50 different plants in this book, there should be plenty left to choose from.

Gardening in general is really good for us. Physical activities such as mowing, pruning, raking, digging planting holes, spreading mulch, and moving pots and soil all help build muscle strength and improve fitness. Gardening can also have a restorative effect on our emotional wellbeing and mental health, with studies showing that 'green time' can help reduce levels of stress and anxiety, and be a mood booster. It also helps foster a connection with nature, which is particularly important as urbanisation increases and green spaces shrink. Whether you have a large sprawling backyard or a tiny balcony or courtyard, gardening is an activity that is open to – and can benefit – everyone. And a gorgeous layer of floral fragrance on top of all that is like icing on the gardening cake!

TOP: Oriental lilies
BOTTOM: Floral perfume

HOW TO CHOOSE WHAT TO GROW

With so many fragrant plants to choose from, how do you begin to narrow down the list, particularly if you have limited space? Here are a few things to consider.

WHAT'S YOUR CLIMATE?

A key driver in deciding what you'll grow is your climate. Sometimes you can find a cosy protected spot in a cool climate that will allow you to grow a warmth-loving plant, or in warm climates you can choose the coolest position in the garden for plants that aren't keen on too much heat. However, plants usually perform best when they're grown in their preferred location.

Whatever your climate zone (cool, temperate or sub-tropical/tropical), there are multiple fragrant options available. Temperate-climate gardeners have the widest choice of fragrant plants; however, some of the best perfumed options for cooler and warmer zones include:

Cool – boronia, buddleja, citrus, daphne, dianthus, jasmine, lavender, lemonwood/tarata, lilac, liliums, lomandra, luculia, magnolias (deciduous and evergreen), Mexican orange blossom, mints, mock orange, port wine magnolia, roses, scented pelargoniums, snail vine, spring- and summer-flowering bulbs, star jasmine, viburnums (deciduous) and wintersweet.

Tropical – alyssum, bouvardia, chocolate cosmos, frangipani, gardenia, heliotrope, jasmine, lemon-scented foliage, liliums, lomandra, Madagascar jasmine, magnolia (evergreen), mints, murraya, native frangipani, rondeletia, sambac jasmine, snail vine, star jasmine, and yesterday today tomorrow.

Together with the different microclimates that can be utilised around a garden, courtyard or balcony, you can be spoilt for fragrant choice, no matter where you live.

The different seasons also play an important role in what to plant and when, because many plants will only reach their potential when planted and grown in their appropriate season. For example, annual (short-lived) sweet peas are usually sown in autumn, grow throughout winter and flower in spring. Whereas frost-tender plants such as murraya are best planted in spring, so they have many months to establish and toughen up before their first winter.

The different seasons also allow a wonderful range of scents and, with some careful plant choices, you can enjoy fragrant flowers and foliage throughout the year. Plant labels and seed packets usually provide helpful information about the preferred climate and best sowing or planting time for your chosen plants.

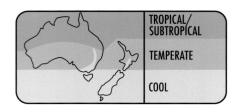

HOW MUCH SPACE DO YOU HAVE?

Big back and front yards will be able to squeeze in lots of fragrant plants. Large trees and shrubs can form the backbone of the garden, interspersed and underplanted with smaller perfumed plants. If you have limited space however, look for dwarf and compact varieties, which take up much less room than their traditional relatives. And get creative with vertical gardens, wall trellises, pots and hanging baskets. A wall covered in a leafy fragrant climber is much nicer to look at than a plain wall and takes up very little room.

Many fragrant plants can be grown in pots and positioned on almost any surface, while hanging baskets – filled with beautiful cascading plants – make the most of thin air! Growing plants in pots has benefits for gardeners with limited mobility, because pots of fragrant plants can be placed in safe and accessible areas and can be elevated to reduce the need for bending. Raised garden beds can also be created for this purpose. Growing plants in pots can also appeal to beginner gardeners, who may find it daunting to embark on a full fragrant-garden design. You can start with just one pot of an easy-care plant and expand from there.

An additional benefit of a potted fragrant garden is that it's portable! People who are renting can take their gardens with them when they move, or plants looking (and smelling) their best can be temporarily moved to where they can be fully appreciated.

Another way to maximise your space and variety of fragrant plants is to grow a few different plants in the one area or container. This works well when the plants are grouped according to their climate preferences, sunlight requirements and watering needs. For example, sun-loving lavender goes together well with dainty honey-scented alyssum, while daphne and luculia both do best in part-shade with cool, moist and well-drained soil.

RIGHT: Small spaces can accommodate lots of plants.

SUN OR SHADE?

What you can grow is heavily influenced by the amount of sunlight you have. Dedicate the spots that receive the most amount of sunlight to your sun-loving plants, and place those plants that tolerate or do best with some shade in the more protected areas. Also observe how the sun changes across the seasons, with the muted winter sun travelling lower in the sky than the intense overhead summer sun.

TOP: Carnations

LEFT: Star jasmine

OPPOSITE: Fragrant plants are
  perfect as borders to paths.

SUN LOVERS

Most flowering plants do best with at least six hours of direct sunshine per day. When grown in a less-than-ideal amount of sun, plants can become sparse and flowering is reduced. Morning sunlight is preferable, because afternoon sunlight is much harsher.

Prioritise these popular fragrant plants for your sunniest spots:

- Citrus
- Frangipani
- Freesias
- Hyacinths
- Jonquils
- Lavender
- Night-scented stock
- Roses
- Snail vine
- Stock
- Sweet peas

LEFT: Lavender
RIGHT: Frangipani

ABOVE: Daphne

TOP LEFT: Lily of the valley

LEFT: Boronia

SHADE-TOLERANT FLOWERS

Partly shaded gardens and outdoor spaces can still have fragrant plants.

Plants that enjoy a partly shady spot include:

- Boronia
- Daphne
- Lily of the valley
- Madagascar jasmine
- Mints

PLANT ATTRIBUTES

Whether you are an experienced gardener or just starting out, have hours to spend in the garden or need quick and low-maintenance options, there's a fragrant plant for you!

BEST PLANTS FOR BEGINNERS

When you're a green thumb in training, it's best to start with some hardy plants. These more forgiving options will help give you confidence before you expand your fragrant plant collection.

Some of the best beginner plants include:

- Alyssum
- Belladonna lily
- Buddleja
- Dianthus
- Freesias
- Jonquils
- Lemonwood/tarata
- Lomandra
- Mexican orange blossom
- Night-scented stock
- Perennial phlox
- Pittosporum
- Scented pelargoniums
- Star jasmine
- Sweet peas
- Viburnums

LEFT: Mexican orange blossom

RIGHT: Buddleja

LOW-MAINTENANCE PLANTS

Pests and diseases can unfortunately plague some plants more than others, while other plants can be quite needy when it comes to water and nutrients.

Here are some low-maintenance plants to include in your garden, which are especially good when you're time-poor or just beginning your gardening journey:

- Alyssum
- Belladonna lily
- Buddleja
- Dianthus
- Freesias
- Jonquils
- Lemonwood/tarata
- Liliums
- Lomandra

- Mock orange
- Murraya
- Osmanthus
- Perennial phlox
- Scented pelargoniums
- Star jasmine
- Sweet rocket
- Viburnums
- Wintersweet

LEFT: Freesias
RIGHT: Murraya

FAST-GROWING PLANTS

We all love quick results and, although plants do take time to reach their full fragrant potential, some are faster than others. For a faster reward of fragrance, look for seedlings, potted colour (almost-mature annuals that are often already in flower), potted biennials and perennials, and semi-mature trees and shrubs in your local garden centre.

Here's a list of the quickest-growing plants that will be rewarding your nose in just a few months:

- Alyssum
- Spring-flowering bulbs – freesias, hyacinths, jonquils, lily of the valley
- Summer- and autumn-flowering bulbs – belladonna lily, liliums, tuberose
- Sweet peas

LEFT: Alyssum
RIGHT: Jonquils

FRAGRANT CUT FLOWERS

A vase of flowers is a real treat and can't help but lift your mood. As an added bonus, fragrant cut flowers help to perfume a room, and they are made all the more special when you have grown them yourself.

These are some of the perfect cut-flower options:

- Annuals – stock, night-scented stock, sweet peas
- Biennials and perennials – chocolate cosmos, dianthus, peonies, perennial phlox, sweet rocket, wallflowers
- Bulbs – belladonna lily, freesias, hyacinths, jonquils, liliums, lily of the valley, tuberose
- Climbers – jasmine, Madagascar jasmine
- Shrubs – boronia, bouvardia, buddleja, gardenia, lavender, lilac, rondeletia, roses

These are the best ways to keep your homegrown cut flowers looking fresh for as long as possible:

- Pick flowers in the cool of the early morning, using sharp secateurs, and immediately plunge the stems into a bucket of cool water.
- Before placing the flowers in a vase filled with cool to tepid water, recut the stem ends on a 45-degree angle. This prevents the stem ends from sitting flat on the base of the vase, which can restrict water uptake.
- Remove any leaves that sit below the water.
- Keep the vase out of direct sunlight and away from draughts.
- Replace the water in the vase every second day.

EVENING FRAGRANCE

As we wind down in the evening, some perfumed plants are moving into top fragrant gear. These plants usually need their flowers pollinated by nocturnal insects and animals, so the plants entice the creatures to their flowers with fragrance as the sun starts to set.

We can benefit from this night-time activity by planting these particular plants around outdoor entertaining areas, or near windows and doors that may be open on warm nights, allowing delightfully perfumed air to drift inside.

Plants that release fragrance during the evenings include:

- Angel's trumpet
- Bouvardia
- Frangipani
- Murraya
- Night-scented stock
- Night-scented tobacco
- Rondeletia
- Sambac jasmine
- Sweet rocket

ABOVE: Frangipani
LEFT: Angel's trumpet

Lilac

SEASONAL FRAGRANCE

The flurry of floral activity in spring is sublime; however, that doesn't mean the rest of the seasons are bereft of colour and fragrance. With some considered choices, you can enjoy perfumed plants almost all year round. As one plant fades, another will come into the fragrant spotlight. Flowering seasons can be influenced by your climate and weather patterns; the diagram opposite will give you an indication of the general flowering times.

SPRING-FLOWERING

Alyssum • Boronia • Buddleja • Citrus
• Dianthus • Freesias • Gardenia • Hyacinths
• Jasmine (early) • Jonquils • Lavender (late)
• Lemonwood/tarata • Lilac • Lily of the valley
• Lomandra • Magnolias (deciduous, early)
• Magnolias (evergreen) • Mexican orange blossom
• Mock orange • Murraya • Native frangipani
• Night-scented stock • Osmanthus • Peonies (late)
• Port wine magnolia • Rondeletia • Roses
• Star jasmine (late) • Stock • Sweet peas
• Wallflowers • Wisteria
• Yesterday today tomorrow

SUMMER-FLOWERING

Alyssum • Angel's trumpet
• Belladonna lily • Bouvardia • Buddleja
• Chocolate cosmos • Dianthus • Frangipani
• Gardenia • Heliotrope • Lavender
• Lemonwood/tarata • Liliums
• Madagascar jasmine • Magnolias (evergreen)
• Mock orange • Murraya • Native frangipani (early)
• Peonies • Perennial phlox • Port wine magnolia
• Roses • Sambac jasmine • Snail vine
• Star jasmine • Stock • Tuberose
• Wallflowers
• Yesterday today tomorrow

WINTER-FLOWERING

Boronia (late) • Daphne
• Jasmine (late)
• Jonquils (late) • Luculia
• Magnolias (deciduous, late)
• Osmanthus • Rondeletia (late)
• Wallflowers • Wintersweet

AUTUMN-FLOWERING

Alyssum • Belladonna lily
• Bouvardia • Carnation • Dianthus
• Gardenia (early) • Luculia
• Roses • Snail vine
• Tuberose

PLANT TYPES

Perfumed plants range from short-lived annuals with a quick burst of colour and scent, to longer-lasting biennials, perennials and bulbs, climbing plants as well as trees, shrubs and plants with fragrant foliage.

ANNUALS

Annuals are plants that usually live for less than a year and flower for a few weeks or months before dying. These short-lived plants are often started from seed, which is an economical way to grow lots of plants. Annuals are a great way to fill out your garden while longer-lived plants establish, and they are also a quick and easy way to create stunning potted seasonal displays.

Fragrant annuals include:

- Alyssum
- Night-scented stock
- Night-scented tobacco
- Stock
- Sweet peas

RIGHT: Sweet peas
BELOW: Stock

LEFT: Wallflower
RIGHT: Peonies

BIENNIALS AND PERENNIALS

Biennials are plants that complete their life cycle in two years, growing in the first year and flowering and setting seed in their second year, before dying. Perennial plants can live for three or more years but, unlike most shrubs, they don't develop woody stems. Perennials can be evergreen, retaining their foliage throughout the seasons, or herbaceous, losing their leaves before dying down in winter and then regrowing in spring. Biennials and perennials are ideal for relatively quick floral results but will persist longer than annuals and help to create a fuller garden. They can be planted among trees and shrubs, grown in combination with annuals or planted in pots. Biennials and perennials can be chosen to flower and provide fragrance at different times of the year.

Scented biennials and perennials include:

- Chocolate cosmos
- Dianthus
- Lomandra
- Peonies

- Perennial phlox
- Sweet rocket
- Wallflowers

BULBS

Bulbs are plants that grow from underground onion-like structures, with leaves and flowers emerging from the bulb. For most bulbs, it takes about 4–6 months for flowers to appear after planting; for example, autumn-planted bulbs will flower in spring.

Depending on the type of bulb, your climate and how the bulbs are grown, bulbs may live for just one year, or may be healthy and robust enough to regrow again at the same time in subsequent years (often referred to as naturalising).

Scented bulbs include:

- Liliums
- Spring-flowering bulbs – freesias, hyacinths, jonquils, lily of the valley
- Summer- and autumn-flowering bulbs – belladonna lily, liliums, tuberose

LEFT: Tuberose
RIGHT: Hyacinth

CLIMBERS

In addition to delightful perfume, climbing plants can offer many wonderful garden benefits, including covering bare walls and fences, creating summer shade and allowing in winter sunshine, having the flexibility to be grown as a ground cover, and helping make the most of often-unused vertical spaces. Climbers can be evergreen or deciduous, delicate or vigorous.

Some of the most fragrant climbers include:

- Jasmine
- Madagascar jasmine
- Sambac jasmine
- Snail vine
- Star jasmine
- Wisteria

Note that sweet peas are also fragrant climbers, but they are included in the Annuals section of this book.

LEFT: Madagascar jasmine
RIGHT: Wisteria

TREES AND SHRUBS

Fragrant trees and shrubs form part of a longer-term garden plan, but are worthwhile inclusions, helping to create garden structure and permanence, as well as offering shade, shelter and privacy. Single trees and large shrubs can also create beautiful garden focal points, particularly when they're smothered in flowers or have striking autumn foliage colours.

Small-space gardens can include trees and shrubs too, because there are numerous compact varieties available, and many are suitable for growing in pots.

Trees and shrubs to consider for your fragrant collection include:

- Angel's trumpet
- Boronia
- Bouvardia
- Buddleja
- Citrus
- Daphne
- Frangipani
- Gardenia
- Heliotrope
- Lavender
- Lemonwood/tarata
- Lilac
- Luculia
- Magnolias (deciduous)
- Magnolias (evergreen)
- Mexican orange blossom
- Mock orange
- Murraya
- Native frangipani
- Osmanthus
- Port wine magnolia
- Rondeletia
- Roses
- Viburnums
- Wintersweet
- Yesterday today tomorrow

TOP: Magnolia
BOTTOM: Gardenia

LEFT: Lemon verbena

RIGHT: Scented pelargoniums

PLANTS WITH FRAGRANT FOLIAGE

Flowers don't have to take all the fragrant glory, with many plants having wonderfully aromatic foliage. Position plants with fragrant foliage alongside pathways, where you can brush past them and release their scent, or grab a handful of leaves as you wander around the garden, lightly crushing them and inhaling their charming aromas.

You can also fill a vase with scented leafy stems. And with fragrant foliage being on hand throughout the year, these plants can help fill the gap between flowering seasons.

Plants with fragrant foliage include:

- Lemon balm
- Lemon myrtle
- Lemon verbena
- Lemongrass
- Mints
- Scented pelargoniums

50 FRAGRANT PLANTS

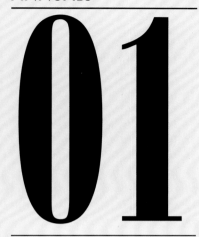

01

DETAILS:

- LOCATION: Cool to tropical; full sun to part-shade

- FLOWERING TIME: Can be year-round; 8 weeks after sowing

- SIZE: 10cm tall x 30cm wide

HIGHLIGHTS:

- Dainty honey-scented flowers

- Ideal garden bed filler

- Quick growing and readily self-seeds

ALYSSUM

Lobularia maritima

Alyssum's flowers might be tiny; however, when grown en masse, they radiate the most wonderful honey-like fragrance. Adored by bees and beneficial insects such as hoverflies and butterflies, alyssum is a hardy, low-growing plant. Although classed as an annual, its ability to self-seed results in new seedlings popping up once the original plant has faded. Also known as sweet Alice, the most common form has pure snowy white flowers, but there are also cream, pink and purple varieties available. Alyssum is easy to grow from seed and is perfect for filling bare spots in the garden or combining with other flowers in pots and hanging baskets.

HOW TO GROW:

For in-ground alyssum:
1. Choose a spot with well-drained soil in full sun to part-shade. Scatter the seeds over the bare soil and cover lightly with seed raising mix.
2. Keep the soil moist and seeds will germinate in 10–14 days. Once established, keep the soil slightly moist.

For potted alyssum:
1. Choose a pot at least 20cm wide that has good drainage holes. Position the pot outdoors in a warm sunny spot.
2. Fill the pot with a quality potting mix. Scatter a few seeds over the potting mix and cover lightly with seed raising mix.
3. Keep the potting mix slightly moist. Alyssum can also be combined in the same pot with other flowers, such as pansies or violas in the cooler seasons or petunias in the warmer seasons.

GROWING TIPS:

- In temperate areas seed can be sown year round, in warm areas during autumn and winter, and in cool areas from spring to autumn. It will take about 8 weeks for seed-sown alyssum to flower.
- Once the seedlings are established, feed every 1–2 weeks with a potassium-rich liquid plant food such as Yates Thrive Rose & Flower Liquid Plant Food.
- Once the plants become leggy or most of the flowers fade, cut back the plants by half to promote fresh growth and more flowers.
- If you would like self-sown alyssum, let some of the plants set seed.

02

DETAILS:
- LOCATION: Cool to sub-tropical; full sun

- FLOWERING TIME: Spring; approx. 20 weeks after sowing

- SIZE: 30–50cm tall x 50cm wide

HIGHLIGHTS:
- Vanilla-like evening fragrance

- Easy to grow from seed

- Pretty annual for cottage gardens and pots

NIGHT-SCENTED STOCK
Matthiola longipetala (syn. Matthiola bicornis)

The common name of this plant reveals when its fragrance peaks! Night-scented stock will fill the garden with sweet vanilla-like perfume during the evening, so be sure to grow these plants around outdoor entertaining areas, or near doors and windows that are open on warm spring and summer evenings. The dainty bee- and butterfly-attracting flowers of this annual are a mix of white, mauve and pink. Night-scented stock is perfectly suited to cottage gardens, where it's best grown en masse or in large clumps. It can also create a pretty potted display. Night-scented stock is most commonly grown from seed, and this is an easy way to get lots of fragrant and pretty plants on a budget.

HOW TO GROW:

For in-ground night-scented stock:
1. Choose a spot with well-drained soil in full sun. Scatter the seeds over the bare soil and cover lightly with seed raising mix.
2. Keep the soil moist and seeds will germinate in 10–14 days. Once established, keep the soil moist but not wet.

For potted night-scented stock:
1. Choose a pot at least 20cm wide that has good drainage holes. Position the pot outdoors in a warm sunny spot where you will be able to enjoy the evening fragrance.
2. Fill the pot with a quality potting mix. Scatter a few seeds over the potting mix and cover lightly with seed raising mix.
3. Keep the potting mix moist while the seeds germinate and establish, and then throughout the growing and flowering seasons.

GROWING TIPS:

- In most areas, sow seed during autumn.
- Once the seedlings are established, feed every 1–2 weeks with a potassium-rich liquid plant food.
- Remove spent flowers regularly to promote further flowering. Some plants can also be left to self-seed.
- Monitor plants for aphid infestation. Consult the pest section for control recommendations.

NIGHT-SCENTED TOBACCO

Nicotiana sylvestris

Evening fragrance is one of the many reasons to grow this tender perennial. Usually treated as an annual, night-scented tobacco has large, lush-looking, slightly sticky leaves as well as tall stems topped with multiple drooping, white, trumpet-shaped flowers that have an aroma similar to jasmine. Grow this interesting plant in the vicinity of windows and doors that are open on summer nights, so you can fully appreciate the after-dusk perfume. Best for growing in garden beds, it's worth seeking out the seeds of this striking but not particularly common plant. Because this plant often self-seeds, you can sow once and enjoy night-scented tobacco for years to come.

HOW TO GROW:

For in-ground night-scented tobacco:
1. Choose a frost-free spot with well-drained soil in full sun to part-shade (flowering will be best in full sun). Scatter the seeds over the bare soil and cover lightly with seed raising mix.
2. Keep the soil moist and seeds will germinate within 3 weeks.
3. Ensure the soil is moist throughout the growing and flowering seasons. Tall stems may need to be supported with stakes in windy areas.

For potted night-scented tobacco:
1. Choose a pot at least 30cm wide that has good drainage holes. Position the pot outdoors in a warm, sunny, wind-protected spot where you will be able to enjoy the evening fragrance.
2. Fill the pot with a quality potting mix. Scatter a few seeds over the potting mix and cover lightly with seed raising mix.
3. Keep the potting mix moist while the seeds germinate and establish, and then throughout the growing and flowering seasons.

DETAILS:

- LOCATION: Cool to sub-tropical; full sun to part-shade

- FLOWERING TIME: Summer to autumn

- SIZE: 1.5–2m tall x 0.5–0.75m wide

HIGHLIGHTS:

- Evening summer fragrance

- White flowers with a jasmine-like perfume

- Ideal for garden beds

GROWING TIPS:

- Sow seeds in spring. Once the seedlings are established, feed every 1–2 weeks with a potassium-rich liquid plant food such as Yates Thrive Rose & Flower Liquid Plant Food.
- Remove spent flowers regularly to promote further flowering. Some plants can also be left to self-seed.
- Night-scented tobacco will continue to flower until the first frosts.
- Monitor plants for insects such as aphids and caterpillars. Consult the pest section for control recommendations.

04

DETAILS:

- LOCATION: Cool to sub-tropical; full sun

- FLOWERING TIME: Spring to summer

- SIZE: 30–60cm tall x 30–40cm wide

HIGHLIGHTS:

- Cottage-garden favourite

- Spicy fragrance reminiscent of cloves

- Exquisite cut flower

STOCK

Matthiola incana

It's hard to believe such a gorgeous-smelling flower is related to cabbages! Stock blooms have a distinctive sweet and spicy clove-like fragrance that has made them cottage-garden favourites for hundreds of years. From 'giant' forms that grow more than 60cm tall to petite varieties half that size, their dense and upright columns of single or double flowers range in colour from bold lavender, red, purple and pink to delicate pastels and white. Best cultivated as annuals and easy to grow from seed, stock provides an economical way to create pretty swathes of fragrant colour in garden beds, gorgeous potted displays or beautiful bunches of cut flowers.

HOW TO GROW:

For in-ground stock:
1. Choose a wind-protected spot with moist but well-drained soil in full sun. Sow the seeds 3mm deep and allow 30cm between plants.
2. Keep the soil moist and seeds will germinate in 10–14 days. Ensure that the soil is moist throughout the growing and flowering seasons.

For potted stock:
1. Choose a pot at least 20cm wide that has good drainage holes. Position the pot outdoors in a warm, sunny, sheltered spot where you will be able to enjoy the flower display and fragrance.
2. Fill the pot with a quality potting mix. Sow a few seeds 3mm deep in the centre of the pot.
3. Keep the potting mix moist while the seeds germinate and establish, and throughout the growing and flowering seasons.

GROWING TIPS:

- In most areas, sow seed from mid-summer to autumn. It will take about 20 weeks for seed-sown stock to flower.
- Once the seedlings are established, feed every 1–2 weeks with a potassium-rich liquid plant food such as Yates Thrive Rose & Flower Liquid Plant Food.
- Protect young seedlings from snails and slugs with a light scattering of snail pellets.
- Monitor plants for signs of powdery mildew. Consult the disease section for control recommendations.

05

DETAILS:

- LOCATION: Cool to sub-tropical; full sun

- FLOWERING TIME: Spring (autumn-sown) or summer (cool-climate spring-sown); 12–14 weeks after sowing

- SIZE: 2m tall (climbing varieties), 50cm tall x 30cm wide (dwarf varieties)

HIGHLIGHTS:

- Easy to grow from seed

- Climbing and compact options

- Wide variety of pretty flower colours

SWEET PEAS

Lathyrus odoratus

Spring-blooming sweet peas are the perfect combination of pretty petals and delightful perfume, and a posy of sweet-pea flowers is simply enchanting. Because they are easy to grow at home from seed sown in autumn, sweet peas should be part of every fragrant garden.

Flower colours include soft and bright pinks, mauve, white, cream and dark maroon, and some have bicolour, flecked or striped petals. Most sweet peas are tall climbers and need a support to grow up; however, there are some low-growing compact varieties that can be planted en masse in a garden bed or grown in a pot or hanging basket.

HOW TO GROW:

For in-ground sweet peas:

1. Choose a spot with moist but well-drained soil in full sun. Climbing sweet peas will need a support to grow up. Sow seeds 25mm deep and 5–7cm apart into moist soil. Do not water them for a few days, because seeds can rot if they are too wet.
2. Seeds will germinate in 10–14 days.
3. Keep the soil moist but not wet until flowering finishes and the leaves start to yellow.

For potted sweet peas:

1. Choose a pot at least 30cm wide that has good drainage holes. Position the pot outdoors in a warm sunny spot where you will be able to enjoy the flower display and fragrance.
2. For climbing sweet peas, insert a tripod into the pot or ensure that the pot is next to a fence with a trellis.
3. Fill the pot with a quality potting mix. Sow seeds 25mm deep and 5–7cm apart into moist potting mix. Do not water them for a few days, as seeds can rot if they are too wet. Seeds will germinate in 10–14 days.
4. Keep the potting mix moist but not wet until flowering finishes and leaves start to yellow.

GROWING TIPS:

- Some sweet peas are more fragrant that others. Seed packets will indicate whether the variety is perfumed.
- In most areas, sow seed during mid- to late autumn.
- Once the seedlings are established, feed every week with a potassium-rich liquid plant food such as Yates Thrive Rose & Flower Liquid Plant Food.
- Protect young seedlings from snails and slugs with a light scattering of snail pellets.
- Monitor plants for signs of powdery mildew. Consult the disease section for control recommendations.
- Regularly pick flowers for a vase display or remove spent flowers, which helps promote further flowering.

06

DETAILS:

- LOCATION: Temperate to tropical; full sun to part-shade
- FLOWERING TIME: Summer
- SIZE: 50cm tall x 40cm wide

HIGHLIGHTS:

- Chocolate scent
- Stunning burgundy blooms
- Delightful cottage-garden perennial

CHOCOLATE COSMOS
Cosmos atrosanguineus

Chocolate cosmos is not a plant that will infuse the garden with sweet perfume, but once you get up close to one of its velvety burgundy flowers, you'll understand why it's a worthy inclusion in this book.

Chocoholics rejoice for – as the name suggests – the blooms smell like chocolate! Native to Mexico, this low-growing perennial makes a wonderful addition to cottage gardens. Its strikingly coloured flowers combine beautifully with pink-, white- and mauve-flowering perennials, as well as plants with silver foliage. Like other cosmos, the flowers attract bees and butterflies, and they can be cut for a vase display.

HOW TO GROW:

For in-ground chocolate cosmos:
1. Choose a frost-free spot with well-drained soil in full sun to part-shade.
2. Dig a hole twice as wide as the plant's root ball and to the same depth. Remove the plant or seedlings from the pot or punnet, place in the hole and backfill with soil, gently firming down around the root ball.
3. Water well to settle the soil around the roots. Chocolate cosmos is tolerant of moderately dry conditions once established but will benefit from being watered thoroughly every 1–2 weeks.

For potted chocolate cosmos:
1. Choose a pot at least 20cm wide that has good drainage holes. Position the pot outdoors in a warm, sunny spot where you can easily enjoy the chocolaty flowers. In cool areas, position the pot against a north-facing wall.
2. Half-fill the pot with a quality potting mix. Remove the plant or seedlings from the original pot or punnet, position in the new pot and backfill gently with potting mix.
3. Water gently to settle the potting mix around the roots. Keep the potting mix slightly moist.

GROWING TIPS:

- Once the plants are established, feed every 1–2 weeks from spring to autumn with a potassium-rich soluble or liquid plant food.
- Remove spent flowers regularly to promote further flowering.
- Chocolate cosmos produces a tuberous root system (similar to dahlias), and mature plants can be divided and replanted in spring.
- Light frost can damage chocolate cosmos; however, plants can reshoot from the tubers in spring.

07

DETAILS:

- LOCATION: Cool to sub-tropical; full sun to part-shade

- FLOWERING TIME: Spring to autumn

- SIZE: 0.2–0.8m tall x 0.2–1m wide

HIGHLIGHTS:

- Spicy aroma that smells like cloves

- Diverse range of flower colours

- Gorgeous cut flower

DIANTHUS

Dianthus spp.

Dianthus is a large genus of plants that includes carnations (*Dianthus caryophyllus*) and plants known as pinks, sweet William and dianthus in general. Usually grown as short-lived perennials, carnations were first mentioned in Greek literature more than 2000 years ago, and people have been enjoying their spicy clove-like fragrance ever since.

Recent plant breeding has seen the introduction of stunning new fragrant varieties in a rainbow of colours. Dianthus plants, which have attractive clumps of evergreen grey-green foliage, are easy to grow in either garden beds or pots. The ability to pick your very own bunch of blooms for a vase makes growing these beauties worthwhile.

HOW TO GROW:

For in-ground dianthus:
1. Choose a spot with well-drained soil (dianthus do not tolerate wet roots) in full sun (morning sun is preferable) to part-shade. Most dianthus are frost-hardy once established.
2. Dig a hole twice as wide as the plant's root ball and to the same depth. Remove the plant or seedlings from the pot or punnet, place in the hole and backfill with soil, gently firming down around the root ball.
3. Water well to settle the soil around the roots. Keep the soil slightly moist.

For potted dianthus:
1. Choose a pot at least 20cm wide that has good drainage holes. Position the pot outdoors in a warm sunny spot where you will be able to enjoy the flower display and fragrance.
2. Half-fill the pot with a quality potting mix. Remove the plant or seedlings from the original pot or punnet, position in the new pot and backfill gently with potting mix.
3. Water gently to settle the potting mix around the roots. Keep the potting mix moist.

GROWING TIPS:

- Once the plants are established, feed every 1–2 weeks with a potassium-rich liquid plant food such as Yates Thrive Rose & Flower Liquid Plant Food.
- Tall-growing varieties may need their flowers supported with stakes.
- Remove spent flowers regularly to promote further flowering.
- Monitor plants for signs of powdery mildew. Consult the disease section for control recommendations.

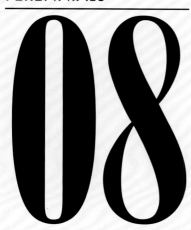

08

DETAILS:

- LOCATION: Cool to tropical; full sun to part-shade

- FLOWERING TIME: Spring

- SIZE: 0.3–0.8m tall x 0.4–0.7m wide

HIGHLIGHTS:

- Hardy, clump-forming, grass-like plants

- Ideal for challenging spots

- Native to Australia

LOMANDRA

Lomandra spp.

Lomandra's perfume will take you by surprise. These Australian native clump-forming plants, such as *Lomandra longifolia* and *Lomandra hystrix*, produce spikes of small creamy-coloured flowers that can often go unnoticed until you walk past and their sweet scent hits you. A word of caution, though, because some types of lomandra have spiny flower heads that you definitely should not bury your nose in! Lomandras are tough and hardy, being drought- and frost-tolerant once established, and many are suited to coastal or damp conditions. They can be grown as edging plants or used to fill challenging garden areas, and their grassy foliage complements plants with large or broad leaves. New compact varieties are available, with some having attractive thin or variegated foliage.

HOW TO GROW:

For in-ground lomandras:
1. Choose a spot in full sun to part-shade.
2. Dig a hole twice as wide as the plant's root ball and to the same depth. Remove the plant from the pot, place in the hole and backfill with soil, gently firming down around the root ball.
3. Water well to settle the soil around the roots. Keep the soil slightly moist while the plant establishes.

For potted lomandras:
1. Compact varieties are best for growing in pots. Choose a pot at least 30cm wide that has good drainage holes. Position the pot in a warm sunny or partly shaded spot, away from where the spiky flower heads could injure you.
2. Half-fill the pot with a quality potting mix. Remove the plant from the original pot, position in the new pot and backfill gently with potting mix.
3. Water gently to settle the potting mix around the roots. Keep the potting mix slightly moist.

GROWING TIPS:

- Check the plant tag of your chosen lomandra for information on its size, best climate and level of fragrance.
- Feed regularly from spring to autumn with a plant food suitable for Australian native plants, such as Yates Dynamic Lifter.
- If required, tidy up the plants by pruning back the foliage.

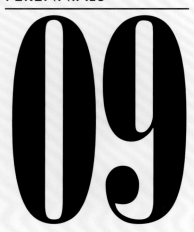

09

DETAILS:

- LOCATION: Cold to cool; full sun to part-shade (tree peonies prefer part-shade)

- FLOWERING TIME: Late spring to summer

- SIZE: 0.7–1m tall x 0.7m wide

HIGHLIGHTS:

- Cool-climate favourites

- Rainbow of flower colours

- Coveted cut flower

PEONIES

Paeonia spp.

Cool- and cold-climate gardeners are fortunate to have the right temperature conditions to grow one of the most coveted of flowers, peonies. Also known as peony roses, their divine rose-like fragrant blooms can be profusely petalled and come in a rainbow of colours, including white and buttery yellow, to almost every shade of pink, from delicate pastel to vivid cerise.

The two most popular peonies are herbaceous and tree peonies. Herbaceous peonies grow into a dense clump of leaves and stems, while tree peonies develop into a small shrub; both types lose their foliage during winter. Once your peonies are well established, you can enjoy cutting their opulent flowers for a vase display.

HOW TO GROW:

For in-ground peonies:

1. Choose a wind-protected spot with fertile, moist but well-drained soil (peonies do not tolerate wet roots) in full sun (morning sun is preferable) to part-shade.
2. Dig a hole twice as wide as the plant's root ball (or rhizome for herbaceous peonies) and to the same depth. Remove the plant or rhizome from the pot or bag, place in the hole and backfill with soil, gently firming down around the root ball or rhizome. The top of the rhizome should sit about 5cm below the soil surface.
3. Water well to settle the soil around the roots or rhizome. Keep the soil moist from spring to autumn.

For potted peonies:

1. Choose a pot at least 30cm wide that has good drainage holes. Position the pot outdoors in a warm, sunny spot where you will be able to enjoy the flower display and fragrance.
2. Half-fill the pot with a quality potting mix. Remove the plant or rhizome from the original pot or bag, position in the new pot and backfill gently with potting mix.
3. Water gently to settle the potting mix around the roots. Keep the potting mix moist from spring to autumn.

GROWING TIPS:

- Rhizomes or potted peonies are best planted in winter; however, potted plants may also be available at other times of the year.
- Peonies need about 3 months of cold conditions during winter to flower well.
- New peony growth in early spring can be damaged by frosts. Protect with a shelter or frost cloth.
- To promote healthy foliage and lots of flowers, feed every 1–2 weeks from spring to early autumn with a potassium-rich liquid plant food such as Yates Thrive Rose & Flower Liquid Plant Food.
- Remove spent flowers regularly. Herbaceous peonies should be cut back to ground level in late autumn once the foliage has browned.
- Peonies do not like to be transplanted, so it's best to plant them in their final position. Only divide and separate congested herbaceous peony clumps after 5 years.

10

DETAILS:

- LOCATION: Cool to temperate; full sun to part-shade

- FLOWERING TIME: Summer

- SIZE: 0.5–1m tall x 0.6m wide

HIGHLIGHTS:

- Perfect in cottage gardens

- Sweet summer fragrance

- Attracts bees and butterflies

PERENNIAL PHLOX

Phlox paniculata

Bees and butterflies will thank you for including perennial phlox in your fragrant collection. They love the sweetly scented blooms on this hardy, clump-forming herbaceous plant, which makes a delightful inclusion in cottage-garden and potted designs. Flower colours include white, purple, orange and pink – some with a darker or different-coloured centre – and the blooms provide colour and fragrance during the warmest months. Perennial phlox's long upright stems make them a perfect cut flower, so be sure to pick pretty bunches for indoors.

HOW TO GROW:

For in-ground perennial phlox:
1. Choose a spot with well-drained soil in full sun (morning sun is preferable) to part-shade.
2. Dig a hole twice as wide as the plant's root ball and to the same depth. Remove the plant or seedlings from the pot or punnet, place in the hole and backfill with soil, gently firming down around the root ball.
3. Water well to settle the soil around the roots. Keep the soil moist.

For potted perennial phlox:
1. Choose a pot at least 20cm wide that has good drainage holes. Position the pot outdoors in a warm sunny spot where you will be able to enjoy the flower display and fragrance.
2. Half-fill the pot with a quality potting mix. Remove the plant or seedlings from the original pot or punnet, position in the new pot and backfill gently with potting mix.
3. Water gently to settle the potting mix around the roots. Keep the potting mix moist.

GROWING TIPS:

- Once the plants are established, feed every 1–2 weeks from spring to autumn with a potassium-rich liquid plant food.
- Remove spent flowers regularly to promote further flowering.
- Cut back plants in late autumn once the foliage has browned.
- Monitor plants for signs of powdery mildew. Consult the disease section for control recommendations.

DETAILS:

- LOCATION: Cool to warm temperate; full sun to part-shade.

- FLOWERING TIME: Spring to summer

- SIZE: 0.5–1m tall x 0.3–0.6m wide

HIGHLIGHTS:

- Sweet aroma in the evening

- Attracts bees and butterflies

- Best grown from seed

SWEET ROCKET

Hesperis matronalis

This hardy biennial is not commonly grown; however, it is worth seeking out to provide warm-season floral colour in cottage gardens and meadow-style plantings. Also known as dame's rocket or dame's violet, a feature of this short-lived plant is its sweet evening fragrance, which is reminiscent of violets. The dainty flowers make perfect cut flowers. They can be white, pink or mauve and are a bee and butterfly favourite. It is best to grow sweet rocket from seed. Once the plants have flowered (in their second year), most will self-seed to provide future perfumed patches of sweet rocket.

HOW TO GROW:

For in-ground sweet rocket:
1. Choose a spot with well-drained soil in full sun or part-shade (plants will flower better in full sun).
2. During spring and summer, scatter the seeds over the bare soil and cover lightly with seed raising mix.
3. Keep the soil moist and seeds will germinate within 21 days. Ensure the soil is moist throughout the growing and flowering seasons.

For potted sweet rocket:
1. Choose a pot at least 20cm wide that has good drainage holes. Position the pot outdoors in a warm, sunny spot where you will be able to enjoy the evening fragrance.
2. Fill the pot with a quality potting mix. Scatter a few seeds over the potting mix and cover lightly with seed raising mix. Water gently.
3. Keep the potting mix moist while the seeds germinate and establish, and then throughout the growing and flowering seasons.

GROWING TIPS:

- Once the seedlings are established, feed every 1–2 weeks with a potassium-rich liquid plant food.
- Remove spent flowers regularly to promote further flowering. Some plants can also be left to self-seed.
- Protect young seedlings from snails and slugs with a light scattering of snail pellets.

12

DETAILS:

- LOCATION: Cool to sub-tropical; full sun to part-shade

- FLOWERING TIME: Winter to summer

- SIZE: 30–75cm tall x 30–75cm wide

HIGHLIGHTS:

- Aroma is both sweet and spicy

- Diverse range of flower colours

- Versatile garden or potted display

WALLFLOWERS

Erysimum spp. (syn. *Cheiranthus* spp.)

Grown as annuals, biennials or perennials, wallflowers have a sweet and spicy fragrance that's a real treat. You can coordinate almost any garden colour scheme with wallflowers; they're available in a rainbow of hues including mauve, pink, apricot, cream, yellow, red and orange. New perennial varieties of wallflowers can flower almost all year round, so you get lots of floral bang for your buck! Wallflowers are perfect for planting in drifts in garden beds, are a fabulous choice for pots and as cut flowers. They are also a valuable source of nectar for bees and other beneficial insects.

HOW TO GROW:

For in-ground wallflowers:
1. Choose a spot with well-drained soil (wallflowers do not tolerate wet roots) in full sun to part-shade.
2. Dig a hole twice as wide as the plant's root ball and to the same depth. Remove the plant or seedlings from the pot or punnet, place in the hole and backfill with soil, gently firming down around the root ball.
3. Water well to settle the soil around the roots. Once established, wallflowers are tolerant of light frosts and moderately dry conditions but will benefit from being watered thoroughly every 1–2 weeks.

For potted wallflowers:
1. Choose a pot at least 20cm wide that has good drainage holes. Position the pot outdoors in a warm, sunny spot where you can enjoy the flowers.
2. Half-fill the pot with a quality potting mix. Remove the plant or seedlings from the original pot or punnet, position in the new pot and backfill gently with potting mix.
3. Water gently to settle the potting mix around the roots. Keep the potting mix slightly moist.

GROWING TIPS:

- Once the plants are established, feed every 1–2 weeks with a potassium-rich liquid plant food.
- Remove spent flowers regularly to promote further flowering.
- Annual wallflowers will need to be replaced each year; biennial wallflowers should last for two years. Perennial wallflowers should be cut back by up to 50 per cent after flowering has finished.

13

DETAILS:

- LOCATION: Cool to warm temperate (Christmas lily), cool to tropical (oriental liliums), cool to tropical (LA Hybrids); full sun to part-shade

- FLOWERING TIME: Summer

- SIZE: Up to 1.2m tall x 0.2–0.3m wide (Christmas lily and oriental liliums), up to 1m tall x 0.2–0.3m wide (LA Hybrids)

HIGHLIGHTS:

- Fragrant summer favourite

- Impressive flower colours and patterns

- Magnificent cut flower

LILIUMS

Lilium spp.

Not all liliums are fragrant; however, we are fortunate to still have a beautiful selection to choose from, when it comes to the perfumed species. *Lilium longiflorum*, known as Christmas lily (or sometimes, confusingly, as Easter or November lily), has long stems topped with scented, trumpet-shaped, pure white flowers in December.

Oriental liliums (Lilium hybrids) come in a breathtaking range of colours and petal patterns, from rich crimson and pale pink to sunshine yellow and white, with multiple superbly fragrant flowers appearing on tall stems during summer.

A third fragrant type of liliums is called LA Hybrids and features hardy plants that are slightly more compact and have vibrantly coloured fragrant flowers. Planted as bulbs during winter or early spring, these three lilium types bring impressive colour and fragrance into the garden in summer.

HOW TO GROW:

For in-ground liliums:
1. Choose a wind-protected spot with well-drained soil (otherwise the bulbs can rot) in full sun (with protection from harsh afternoon sun) to part-shade.
2. During winter and early spring, plant bulbs 15cm deep and 30cm apart. Bulbs look best when planted in groups of three or more.
3. Keep the soil slightly moist during the growing and flowering seasons.

For potted liliums:
1. Choose a pot at least 20cm wide that has good drainage holes. Position the pot outdoors in a warm sunny spot.
2. Fill the pot with a quality potting mix. Dig a 15cm-deep hole in the centre of the pot, plant one bulb and cover with potting mix. Pots larger than 20cm can accommodate more bulbs.
3. Keep the potting mix slightly moist throughout the growing and flowering seasons.

Christmas lily

Oriental lily

GROWING TIPS:

- From when the foliage starts to emerge until the leaves die down, feed every 1–2 weeks with a potassium-rich liquid plant food such as Yates Thrive Rose & Flower Liquid Plant Food.
- In well-drained soil, lilies can be left in the ground to multiply. Every few years, congested clumps can be lifted and separated in early winter.
- Protect new bulb foliage from snails and slugs with a light scattering of snail pellets.
- To promote the best bulb health, do not cut back the foliage before it has completely died down.
- Lilies are toxic if consumed by humans or pets, particularly cats.
- When using lilies as cut flowers, choose blooms that have only just started to open. In the early morning, cut off one-third to half of the stem and remove the leaves from the lower part of the stem. Carefully removing the anthers (that contain pollen) from the centre of the flowers can help prevent the petals (and furniture) from being stained.

14

DETAILS:

- LOCATION: Cool to temperate (jonquils and freesias will tolerate warmer areas); full sun (freesias, hyacinths and jonquils), to part-shade (lily of the valley)
- FLOWERING TIME: Late winter to spring
- SIZE: up to 40cm tall and wide

HIGHLIGHTS:

- Delightful spring fragrance
- Gorgeous range of flower colours
- Ideal for garden and potted displays

SPRING-FLOWERING BULBS: FREESIAS, HYACINTHS, JONQUILS, LILY OF THE VALLEY

Freesia x hybrida, Hyacinthus orientalis, Narcissus tazetta, Convallaria majalis

Late winter- and spring-blooming bulbs and rhizomes are a delightful surprise after being planted many months earlier. Freesias are very popular because they are easy to grow. They have vibrantly coloured flowers and a delightful super-sweet fragrance. Hyacinths produce a flower spike densely covered in superbly fragrant flowers of pink, mauve, purple, blue, white or yellow. Related to daffodils, jonquils are some of the earliest bulbs to flower in late winter and have stalks with multiple single or double blooms in white, cream and yellow. Some people adore the strong smell of jonquils, while others find them overpowering. And lily of the valley has sprays of gorgeous little white or pink bell-shaped flowers. Its jasmine-like fragrance is included in many perfumes and essential oils.

HOW TO GROW:

For in-ground spring-flowering bulbs:
1. Choose a spot with moist but well-drained soil in full sun (or part-shade for lily of the valley).
2. During autumn, plant freesia bulbs 7cm deep, hyacinth and jonquil bulbs 12cm deep, and lily of the valley rhizomes 2cm deep. Plant freesias, jonquils and lily of the valley 10cm apart and hyacinths 15cm apart.
3. Avoid overwatering because this can rot the bulbs. Once the foliage emerges, keep the soil slightly moist until it dies down at the end of spring.

For potted spring-flowering bulbs:
1. Choose a pot at least 20cm wide that has good drainage holes. Position the pot outdoors in a warm, sunny spot (or partly shaded area for lily of the valley).
2. Half-fill the pot with a quality potting mix. Arrange the bulbs on the surface of the potting mix and then cover potting mix until the bulbs are planted at their correct depth.
3. Keep the potting mix slightly moist from when the foliage first emerges until it dies down at the end of spring.

CLOCKWISE FROM TOP LEFT: Freesias; hyacinths, jonquils, lily of the valley

---

GROWING TIPS:

- Hyacinth bulbs should be chilled for 6 weeks in the crisper section of the refrigerator before planting.
- Protect new bulb foliage from snails and slugs with a light scattering of snail pellets.
- From when the leaves appear until the foliage browns in late spring, feed every 1–2 weeks with a potassium-rich liquid plant food such as Yates Thrive Rose & Flower Liquid Plant Food.
- To promote the best bulb health, do not cut back the foliage before it has completely died down.
- In cool to temperate climates, freesias and jonquils can be left in the ground to naturalise. It is best to lift hyacinths each year.
- Hyacinths can also be grown in a brightly lit spot indoors in a special vase, where the bulb is suspended above water.

15

DETAILS:

- LOCATION: Cool to tropical; full sun to part-shade

- FLOWERING TIME: Late summer to early autumn

- SIZE: Up to 120cm tall x 20cm wide (tuberose), up to 60cm tall x 60cm wide (belladonna lily)

HIGHLIGHTS:

- Tuberose has a gardenia-like perfume

- Belladonna lily is a hardy bulb

- Beautiful cut flowers

SUMMER- AND AUTUMN-FLOWERING BULBS:
TUBEROSE, BELLADONNA LILY

Agave amica (syn. Polianthes tuberosa), Amaryllis belladonna

Spring doesn't get all the fragrant bulbs, with gorgeous tuberose and belladonna lily flowering in late summer and early autumn. Tuberose grows a tall flower spike topped with multiple small white flowers. With an intense scent reminiscent of gardenias, tuberose is popular in bridal displays and is also a common note in perfumes. Belladonna lilies are also known as naked ladies, because their bare flower spikes emerge in late summer before any foliage. It is a hardy plant with clusters of large trumpet-shaped flowers in pink or white that have a strong sweet scent. The robust flower stems are ideal for a vase.

HOW TO GROW:

For in-ground summer- and autumn-flowering bulbs:

1. Choose a spot with moist but well-drained soil in full sun to part-shade.
2. During early spring, plant tuberose bulbs 5cm deep and 10cm apart. Throughout spring, plant belladonna lily bulbs with the top of the bulb just above the soil surface and 20cm apart. Bulbs looks best when planted in groups of three or more.
3. Avoid overwatering – this can rot the bulbs. Once the foliage or belladonna lily flower stem emerges, keep the soil slightly moist until the plant dies down.

For potted summer- and autumn-flowering bulbs:

1. Choose a pot at least 20cm wide that has good drainage holes. Position the pot outdoors in a warm, sunny spot.
2. Fill the pot with a quality potting mix. For tuberose, dig 5cm-deep holes 10cm apart. For belladonna lily, dig holes deep enough so that the top of the bulb remains exposed. One belladonna lily can be grown in a 20cm-diameter pot.
3. Keep the potting mix slightly moist from when the foliage or belladonna lily flower stem first emerges until the plant dies down.

Tuberose

Belladonna lily

GROWING TIPS:

- Being a tall plant, tuberose will do best in a spot sheltered from strong winds.
- Protect new bulb foliage from snails and slugs with a light scattering of snail pellets.
- From when the foliage or flower stem starts to emerge until the leaves die down, feed every 1–2 weeks with a potassium-rich liquid plant food such as Yates Thrive Rose & Flower Liquid Plant Food.
- To promote the best bulb health, do not cut back the foliage before it has completely died down.
- In well-drained soil, tuberose and belladonna lily bulbs can be left in the ground to multiply. Every few years, congested clumps of tuberose can be lifted and separated in early winter and belladonna lily in spring.
- Belladonna lily is toxic if consumed by humans or pets.

16

DETAILS:

- LOCATION: Cool temperate to tropical; full sun to part-shade

- FLOWERING TIME: Late winter to early spring

- SIZE: Stems can grow up to 6m long

HIGHLIGHTS:

- Pretty pink buds and white flowers from late winter

- Magnificent fragrance

- Keep growth under control in a pot

JASMINE
Jasminum polyanthum

There are many different species of jasmine, but the one people are most familiar with is *Jasminum polyanthum*. Known as pink jasmine or simply jasmine, its flowers have the most exquisitely sweet fragrance. It heralds spring, being one of the first plants to flower from late winter, and its climbing stems are covered first in clusters of pretty pale pink buds followed by small, white, five-petalled flowers. Due to its fast and vigorous growth, this jasmine is classed as a weed in many areas. However, it can be grown responsibly by keeping it well tamed or growing it in a pot, and not disposing of stems in bushland.

HOW TO GROW:

For in-ground jasmine:
1. Choose a frost-free spot with well-drained soil in full sun to part-shade, next to a trellis or support.
2. Dig a hole twice as wide as the plant's root ball and to the same depth.
3. Remove the plant from the pot, place in the hole and backfill with soil, gently firming down around the root ball.
4. Water well to settle the soil around the roots. Keep the soil moist.

For potted jasmine:
1. Choose a pot at least 30cm wide that has good drainage holes. Position the pot outdoors in a frost-free sunny or partly shaded spot. In cool areas, position the pot against a protected north-facing wall.
2. Half-fill the pot with a quality potting mix. Insert a tripod or sturdy support in the pot. Remove the plant from the original pot, position in the new pot and backfill gently with potting mix.
3. Water gently to settle the potting mix around the roots. Keep the potting mix moist.

GROWING TIPS:

- To promote healthy foliage and lots of flowers, feed every week from autumn to spring with a potassium-rich liquid plant food such as Yates Thrive Rose & Flower Liquid Plant Food.
- Once established, jasmine is tolerant of light frosts.
- Prune back spent flower stems and regularly cut back excessive growth.
- Cut fragrant flowering stems for a vase display.

17

DETAILS:
- LOCATION: Warm temperate to tropical; part-shade
- FLOWERING TIME: Summer
- SIZE: Twining stems can grow up to 6m long

HIGHLIGHTS:
- Gorgeous cut flower
- Exquisitely fragrant white blooms
- Ideal for a shady spot in warm climates

MADAGASCAR JASMINE

Marsdenia floribunda (syn. Stephanotis floribunda)

Madagascar jasmine is an evergreen climber that has fast-growing, long, twining stems with leathery green leaves and clusters of intensely perfumed, white, tubular flowers during summer. The blooms are a favourite in bridal bouquets, are particularly vase-worthy or can be floated in a bowl of water to scent a room. Needing a warm to hot and humid climate to flourish (like their native Madagascar), potted plants can be brought indoors for the winter in cooler areas.

HOW TO GROW:

For in-ground Madagascar jasmine:
1. Choose a frost-free, wind-protected, warm spot with well-drained soil in part-shade (morning sun and afternoon shade is ideal), next to a trellis or support.
2. Dig a hole twice as wide as the plant's root ball and to the same depth.
3. Remove the plant from the pot, place in the hole and backfill with soil, gently firming down around the root ball.
4. Water well to settle the soil around the roots. Keep the soil moist.

For potted Madagascar jasmine:
1. Choose a pot at least 30cm wide that has good drainage holes. Position the pot outdoors in a frost-free, warm, partly shaded spot. Morning sun and afternoon shade is ideal.
2. Half-fill the pot with a quality potting mix. Insert a sturdy support in the pot (or position the pot next to a fence with a wire trellis). Remove the plant from the original pot, position in the new pot and backfill gently with potting mix.
3. Water gently to settle the potting mix around the roots. Keep the potting mix moist. Plants can be kept in the same pot for several years and don't mind becoming a little root-bound.

GROWING TIPS:

- To promote healthy foliage and lots of flowers, feed every 1–2 weeks from spring to autumn with a potassium-rich liquid plant food such as Yates Thrive Rose & Flower Liquid Plant Food.
- If trimming is required, prune back stems after flowering has finished. This will help to encourage bushier growth.
- Monitor plants for insects such as mealybugs and mites. Consult the pest section for control recommendations.
- Mature Madagascar jasmine can produce large, pear-shaped, inedible fruit.

18

SAMBAC JASMINE

Jasminum sambac

Sambac jasmine's flowers are so beautifully fragrant that they are often distilled into essential oils. Also known as Arabian jasmine, this evergreen scrambling climber produces clusters of small, white, waxy flowers during summer. It's particularly fragrant at night, so is ideal for planting around summer outdoor entertaining areas or next to windows that are left open in the evening, allowing in a gentle sweetly perfumed breeze. Native to tropical Asia, it makes a lovely inclusion in warm, frost-free gardens and can also be grown in a pot. A popular cultivar of sambac jasmine is 'Grand Duke of Tuscany', which has larger double flowers and can bloom throughout the year in warm climates.

DETAILS:

- LOCATION: Warm temperate to tropical; full sun to part-shade
- FLOWERING TIME: Summer
- SIZE: 2–3m tall x 2–3m wide

HIGHLIGHTS:

- Sweet fragrance on summer evenings
- Ideal for warm climates
- Grow as a climber or a shrub

HOW TO GROW:

For in-ground sambac jasmine:
1. Choose a frost-free spot with well-drained soil in full sun to part-shade, next to a trellis or support.
2. Dig a hole twice as wide as the plant's root ball and to the same depth.
3. Remove the plant from the pot, place in the hole and backfill with soil, gently firming down around the root ball.
4. Water well to settle the soil around the roots. Keep the soil moist.

For potted sambac jasmine:
1. Choose a pot at least 30cm wide that has good drainage holes. Position the pot outdoors in a warm sunny or frost-free partly shaded spot.
2. Half-fill the pot with a quality potting mix. Insert a sturdy support in the pot (or position the pot next to a fence with a wire trellis). Remove the plant from the original pot, position in the new pot and backfill gently with potting mix.
3. Water gently to settle the potting mix around the roots. Keep the potting mix moist.

GROWING TIPS:

- To promote healthy foliage and lots of flowers, feed every 1–2 weeks from spring to autumn with a potassium-rich liquid plant food.
- Sambac jasmine can be kept trimmed as a rambling shrub or trained up a support or fence.
- Pruning is best done after flowering, which will also help promote bushier growth.

19

DETAILS:

- LOCATION: Cool to tropical; full sun

- FLOWERING TIME: Summer to autumn

- SIZE: Stems can grow many metres long

HIGHLIGHTS:

- Fascinating spiral flowers

- Sweetly scented

- Quick-growing climber

SNAIL VINE

Vigna caracalla

Once you see the fascinating flowers on this evergreen tropical-looking climber, you'll understand why it's called snail vine. The clusters of gorgeous spiral flowers – which start green, white and mauve, and then mature to pink and creamy yellow – resemble the corkscrew pattern on a snail's shell. The fragrance is divine and is reminiscent of wisteria, jasmine and hyacinths. It's a wonderful, fast-growing, leafy climber that can quickly cover a fence or twine up a pergola or over an archway. Small-space gardeners don't need to miss out, because snail vine is also perfect for growing in a pot.

HOW TO GROW:

For in-ground snail vine:
1. Choose a spot with well-drained soil in full sun, next to a support.
2. Dig a hole twice as wide as the plant's root ball and to the same depth.
3. Remove the plant from the pot, place in the hole and backfill with soil, gently firming down around the root ball.
4. Water well to settle the soil around the roots. Keep the soil moist.

For potted snail vine:
1. Choose a pot at least 30cm wide that has good drainage holes. Position the pot outdoors in a sunny spot.
2. Half-fill the pot with a quality potting mix. Insert a strong tripod or sturdy support in the pot or position the pot next to a fence or trellis. Remove the plant from the original pot, position in the new pot and backfill gently with potting mix.
3. Water gently to settle the potting mix around the roots. Keep the potting mix moist.

GROWING TIPS:

- In cooler areas, snail vine can die back or lose its leaves in winter. Young snail vines should be protected from frost.
- To promote healthy foliage and lots of flowers, feed every 1–2 weeks from spring to autumn with a potassium-rich liquid plant food.
- After flowering, prune back stems to the required size.
- Don't be alarmed if you see ants in the flowers – snail-vine flowers are pollinated by ants. If pea-like seed pods are produced, the seeds can be used to grow more plants.

20

DETAILS:

- LOCATION: Cool to tropical; full sun to part-shade

- FLOWERING TIME: Late spring to summer

- SIZE: Stems can grow up to 5m long

HIGHLIGHTS:

- Intense fragrance

- Hardy climber or ground cover

- Ideal for covering a bare wall

STAR JASMINE

Trachelospermum jasminoides

Star jasmine's heavenly heady fragrance will greet you long before you spot the plant itself. Masses of small, white, five-petalled flowers appear in late spring and summer, lasting for many weeks.

It's a hardy evergreen climber with dark green leaves, which can be planted next to a trellis or wires attached to a wall (it's ideal for covering a less-than-attractive fence in dense leafy growth) or trained up and over a pergola or arch. It can also be left to grow as a 50cm-tall, sprawling ground cover or planted in pots, so even the tiniest gardens can enjoy this sensational plant.

HOW TO GROW:

For in-ground star jasmine:
1. Choose a spot with well-drained soil in full sun to part-shade, next to a support if the plant is to be grown as a climber.
2. Dig a hole twice as wide as the plant's root ball and to the same depth.
3. Remove the plant from the pot, place in the hole and backfill with soil, gently firming down around the root ball.
4. Water well to settle the soil around the roots. Keep the soil moist.

For potted star jasmine:
1. Choose a pot at least 30cm wide that has good drainage holes. Position the pot outdoors in a warm sunny or partly shaded spot.
2. Half-fill the pot with a quality potting mix. Insert a sturdy support in the pot (or position the pot next to a fence with a wire trellis) if the plant is to be grown as a climber.
3. Remove the plant from the original pot, position in the new pot and backfill gently with potting mix.
4. Water gently to settle the potting mix around the roots. Keep the potting mix moist.

GROWING TIPS:

- To promote healthy foliage and lots of flowers, feed from spring to autumn with a potassium-rich plant food such as Yates Thrive Rose & Flower Plant Food.
- To keep star jasmine to the desired size, or create a more formal look, prune back stems after flowering has finished. This will also help promote bushier growth.
- Star jasmine is also available in a variegated variety (*Trachelospermum jasminoides* 'Tricolour'), which has a pretty combination of green, cream and pink foliage.
- Star jasmine is tolerant of light frosts once established.

21

DETAILS:
- LOCATION: Cold to sub-tropical; full sun to part-shade
- FLOWERING TIME: Spring
- SIZE: Stems can grow many metres long

HIGHLIGHTS:
- Clusters of mauve, white or pink flowers
- Perfect for covering a pergola
- Hardy, vigorous, deciduous climber

WISTERIA
Wisteria spp.

Wisteria is adored for its (most commonly) fragrant mauve flowers, which hang grape-like from the vines. A fast-growing, frost- and drought-hardy deciduous climber, wisteria is ideal for growing over pergolas to create a mesmerising ceiling of pendulous flowers and summer shade, or creating a leafy cover over fences.

Two of the most common forms of wisteria grown in home gardens are the prolific Japanese wisteria (*Wisteria floribunda*), which is also available in white and pink forms, and Chinese wisteria (*Wisteria sinensis*), which has slightly shorter flower clusters.

HOW TO GROW:

For in-ground wisteria:
1. Choose a spot with well-drained soil in full sun to part-shade, next to a very sturdy support, fence or pergola.
2. Dig a hole twice as wide as the plant's root ball and to the same depth. Enrich the soil dug from the hole with an organic soil improver such as Yates Dynamic Lifter.
3. Remove the plant from the pot, place in the hole and backfill with soil, gently firming down around the root ball.
4. Water well to settle the soil around the roots. Keep the soil moist from spring to autumn.

For potted wisteria:
1. Choose a pot at least 40cm wide that has good drainage holes. Position the pot outdoors in a sunny or partly shaded spot.
2. Half-fill the pot with a quality potting mix. Insert a strong tripod in the pot (or position the pot next to a support for the plant to climb up). Remove the plant from the original pot, position in the new pot and backfill gently with potting mix.
3. Water gently to settle the potting mix around the roots. Keep the potting mix moist from spring to autumn.

GROWING TIPS:

- Wisteria can be planted year-round, including in winter while dormant.
- Because wisteria is a very vigorous and heavy climber, choosing a growing position requires careful consideration. Wisteria should not be allowed to grow up and into a tree (because this can weaken the tree) or climb over buildings that could be damaged.
- To keep the plant manageable and prevent it from growing into unintended areas, prune wisteria stems back after flowering has finished. Also remove any suckers.
- Wisteria can be grown into a feature 'tree' by training it up a strong central pole that has a horizontal wheel-shaped support on the top; it can also be grown as a bonsai.

22

DETAILS:

- LOCATION: Warm temperate to sub-tropical; full sun to part-shade

- FLOWERING TIME: Late spring to summer

- SIZE: 3–6m tall x 1–4m wide

HIGHLIGHTS:

- Rich evening fragrance

- Striking pendulous flowers

- Can flower year round in warm climates.

ANGEL'S TRUMPET

Brugmansia spp.

Angel's trumpets are fast-growing sub-tropical trees or large shrubs native to South America. They have pendulous, trumpet-shaped, single or ruffled double flowers in shades of pink, white, apricot and yellow, with a rich sweet scent. As the fragrance is strongest at night, they're ideal for growing around outdoor entertaining areas, or near windows and doors that are open during hot summer nights, allowing the fragrance to drift indoors. Important note: all parts of angel's trumpets are poisonous, including the sap and seeds, to both humans and pets; take care when handling the plants.

HOW TO GROW:

For in-ground angel's trumpet:
1. Choose a frost-free, wind-protected spot with well-drained soil in full sun (with protection from the harsh afternoon sun) to part-shade.
2. Dig a hole twice as wide as the plant's root ball and to the same depth. Remove the plant from the pot, place in the hole and backfill with soil, gently firming down around the root ball.
3. Water well to settle the soil around the roots. Though drought-hardy once established, they'll do best when watered thoroughly and deeply once every 1–2 weeks from spring to autumn.

For potted angel's trumpet:
1. Choose a pot at least 50cm wide that has good drainage holes. Position the pot outdoors in a warm, sunny spot protected from wind and frost.
2. Half-fill the pot with a quality potting mix. Remove the plant from the original pot, position in the new pot and backfill gently with potting mix.
3. Water gently to settle the potting mix around the roots. Keep the potting mix slightly moist.

GROWING TIPS:

- Prune during winter to limit the plant's size.
- Angel's trumpet strikes readily from hardwood cuttings during winter.
- To promote healthy foliage and lots of flowers, feed regularly from spring to autumn with a potassium-rich plant food.
- Monitor plants for insects such as mealybugs, whiteflies, aphids and spider mites. Consult the pest section for control recommendations.
- Some species of angel's trumpet are not fragrant – check the plant tag for information.

23

DETAILS:
- LOCATION: Cool to tropical (depending on the type); full sun

- FLOWERING TIME: Spring

- SIZE: 1.5–5m tall x 1–4m wide (dwarf trees are more compact)

HIGHLIGHTS:
- Lots of sweetly scented white flowers

- Dwarf varieties are ideal for pots

- Double benefit of delicious fruit

CITRUS
Citrus spp.

Because we're understandably distracted by the colourful and delicious citrus fruit, we often forget that citrus blossoms are divine. Masses of fragrant white flowers emerge in spring, delighting the bees and perfuming the air. An example of the fragrant value of citrus flowers is the essential oil neroli, which is distilled from flowers of the bitter orange (*Citrus x aurantium*).

Grapefruit and lemons also have beautifully fragrant flowers; however, the blooms on sweet oranges, such as navel and Valencia, are particularly captivating. Choose a citrus tree that's suited to your climate (and your tastebuds!).

HOW TO GROW:

For in-ground citrus:
1. Choose a warm, frost-free spot with well-drained soil (citrus do not tolerate wet roots) in full sun. Meyer lemons will tolerate cool climates and light frosts once established.
2. Dig a hole twice as wide as the plant's root ball and to the same depth. Enrich the soil dug from the hole with an organic soil improver such as Yates Dynamic Lifter.
3. Remove the plant from the pot, place in the hole and backfill with soil, gently firming down around the root ball.
4. Water well to settle the soil around the roots. Keep the soil moist but not wet.

For potted citrus:
1. Dwarf varieties of citrus are best for pots. Choose a pot at least 40cm wide that has good drainage holes. Position the pot outdoors in a frost-free, warm, sunny spot. In cool areas, position the pot against a warm, protected, north-facing wall.
2. Half-fill the pot with a quality potting mix. Remove the plant from the original pot, position in the new pot and backfill gently with potting mix.
3. Water gently to settle the potting mix around the roots. Keep the potting mix moist but not wet.

Valencia oranges

GROWING TIPS:

- To promote health foliage and lots of flowers (and fruit), feed throughout the year with a specialised citrus food such as Yates Thrive Citrus & Fruit Plant Food.
- Plant labels provide information on the best climate for that particular citrus tree. For example, Tahitian limes prefer warm climates.
- The unusually shaped fruit of Buddha's hand (*Citrus medica* var. *sarcodactylis*) is also intensely fragrant, and a bowl of fruit can scent a room.
- Bergamot oil, a popular essential oil and fragrance, is extracted from the rind of the bergamot orange (*Citrus bergamia*).
- Monitor plants for insects such as aphids and scale. Consult the pest section for control recommendations.

FRANGIPANI

Plumeria spp.

If there's one tree that can transport you back to a dreamy tropical-island holiday, it's the frangipani. Native to Central America, frangipanis are deciduous or semi-evergreen umbrella-shaped trees with large leathery leaves and clusters of sweetly scented waxy flowers; the perfume is strongest at night.

There is a dazzling array of flower colours now available, from traditional white with a yellow centre, to many shades of pink, yellow, salmon, crimson and red, some with beautiful multicoloured petals. They're wonderful trees for providing cooling shade and gorgeous flowers in summer.

DETAILS:

- LOCATION: Temperate to tropical; full sun

- FLOWERING TIME: Late spring to early autumn in temperate areas, year-round in the tropics

- SIZE: 2–8m tall x 1.5–5m wide

HIGHLIGHTS:

- Stunning variety of flower colours

- Beautiful fragrance

- Suits a tropical-style garden

HOW TO GROW:

For in-ground frangipani:

1. Choose a frost-free spot with well-drained soil (frangipanis do not tolerate poorly drained soil) in full sun.
2. Dig a hole twice as wide as the plant's root ball and to the same depth. Enrich the soil dug from the hole with an organic soil improver such as Yates Dynamic Lifter.
3. Remove the plant from the pot, place in the hole and backfill with soil, gently firming down around the root ball.
4. Water well to settle the soil around the roots. Keep the soil slightly moist from spring to autumn.
5. Frangipanis are drought-tolerant once established, but they do best with deep watering during dry conditions.

For potted frangipani:

1. Dwarf varieties of frangipani are best for pots. Choose a pot at least 40cm wide that has good drainage holes. Position the pot outdoors in a frost-free, warm, sunny spot.
2. Half-fill the pot with a quality potting mix. Remove the plant from the original pot, position in the new pot and backfill gently with potting mix.
3. Water gently to settle the potting mix around the roots. Keep the potting mix slightly moist from spring to autumn.

GROWING TIPS:

- Frangipanis are commonly available during summer but are ideally planted in winter while dormant.
- To promote healthy foliage and lots of flowers, feed regularly from spring to autumn with a potassium-rich plant food such as Yates Thrive Rose & Flower Plant Food.
- Individual flowers can be brought inside and floated in a shallow bowl of water.
- Frangipanis can be grown from stem cuttings taken in late spring. Take a 30cm piece of stem, remove most of the leaves and let it dry out for a few weeks before inserting the stem 10cm deep into pot of slightly moist potting mix. Roots can take several months to develop.
- Monitor plants for signs of rust disease, which appears as orange powdery spots on the underside of leaves. Consult the disease section for control recommendations.

DETAILS:

- LOCATION: Cool to sub-tropical; full sun to part-shade

- FLOWERING TIME: Spring to summer

- SIZE: 6–12m tall x 4–5m wide

HIGHLIGHTS:

- Doubly fragrant – foliage and flowers

- Attracts birds and bees

- New Zealand native

LEMONWOOD/TARATA

Pittosporum eugenioides

Pittosporums are common garden inclusions, because they make fantastic fast-growing hedges. One species in particular, *Pittosporum eugenioides* – known as the lemonwood or tarata – is native to New Zealand and has dual fragrances: lemon-scented leaves and flowers that smell like honey.

The evergreen, dense, wavy-edged foliage provides a wonderful screen, and the plants can be trimmed into formal or informal hedges. Crush handfuls of leaves to release the delightful lemony fragrance. Appearing from mid-spring, birds and bees love the small creamy-coloured flowers. Tolerant of light frosts as well as coastal and windy conditions, the hardy lemonwood/tarata is an ideal choice when you need a quick-growing screen.

HOW TO GROW:

For in-ground lemonwood/tarata:

1. Choose an appropriately sized spot with well-drained soil in full sun to part-shade.
2. Dig a hole twice as wide as the plant's root ball and to the same depth. Remove the plant from the pot, place in the hole and backfill with soil, gently firming down around the root ball.
3. Water well to settle the soil around the roots. Keep the soil moist.

Note: lemonwood/tarata grows too large to plant in a pot.

GROWING TIPS:

- Protect young plants from frost.
- There is an attractive variegated version of the lemonwood/tarata that has leaves with creamy-coloured markings.
- Monitor plants for insects such as scale. Consult the pest section for control recommendations.
- Prune the trees as required after flowering.
- To promote healthy foliage and lots of flowers, feed regularly from spring to autumn.

26

MAGNOLIAS (DECIDUOUS)

Magnolia spp.

Deciduous magnolias make magnificent feature trees, providing beautiful flowers, summer shade and colourful autumn foliage. During late winter and early spring, the bare branches of deciduous magnolias are adorned with stunning, large, goblet-shaped flowers in a range of gorgeous colours from deep burgundy to multiple shades of pink, as well as yellow and white.

Some of these deciduous magnolias are fragrant, including Magnolia 'Heaven Scent' (*Magnolia liliiflora* x *veitchii*), with delightful pale pink flowers; Magnolia 'Star Wars' (*Magnolia liliiflora* x *campbellii*), with dark pink flowers; and *Magnolia stellata*, which is a small tree growing to 3m tall with masses of delicately scented, star-shaped white or pink flowers.

DETAILS:

- LOCATION: Cool to temperate; full sun to part-shade

- FLOWERING TIME: Late winter to early spring

- SIZE: 3–8m tall x 2–8m wide

HIGHLIGHTS:

- Striking goblet-shaped flowers

- Diverse range of flower colours

- Beautiful feature trees

HOW TO GROW:

For in-ground deciduous magnolias:
1. Choose an appropriately sized, wind-protected spot with well-drained soil in full sun to part-shade.
2. Dig a hole twice as wide as the plant's root ball and to the same depth. Enrich the soil dug from the hole with an organic soil improver such as Yates Dynamic Lifter.
3. Remove the plant from the pot, place in the hole and backfill with soil, gently firming down around the root ball.
4. Water well to settle the soil around the roots. Keep the soil moist from spring to autumn.

For potted deciduous magnolias:
1. Dwarf varieties of deciduous magnolias are best for pots. Choose a pot at least 40cm wide that has good drainage holes. Position the pot outdoors in a warm, wind-protected, sunny spot.
2. Half-fill the pot with a quality potting mix. Remove the plant from the original pot, position in the new pot and backfill gently with potting mix.
3. Water gently to settle the potting mix around the roots. Keep the potting mix moist from spring to autumn.

GROWING TIPS:

- Deciduous magnolias are best planted during winter while they are dormant; however, potted magnolias can also be planted during spring.
- Deciduous magnolias prefer a slightly acidic soil. In areas with alkaline soil, apply liquid sulfur to lower the soil pH.
- It's best to avoid pruning magnolias, because this can spoil the look of the tree.
- To promote healthy foliage and lots of flowers, feed regularly from spring to autumn with a potassium-rich plant food.
- Magnolias are frost-tolerant once established.

27

DETAILS:
- LOCATION: Cool to tropical (depending on the species and variety); full sun to part-shade
- FLOWERING TIME: Spring to summer (depending on the species and variety)
- SIZE: 4–10m tall x 2–8m wide

HIGHLIGHTS:
- Versatile range of trees and shrubs
- Wonderful as shade trees or fragrant hedges
- Compact varieties suitable for pots

MAGNOLIAS (EVERGREEN)
Magnolia spp.

Evergreen magnolias range from large trees to tall shrubs, so there's a magnolia for almost every garden size. Evergreen magnolias predominantly have white flowers; however, there are newer varieties with pretty pink or cream blooms.

Some of the most popular fragrant evergreen magnolias include the spring-flowering Himalayan evergreen magnolia (*Magnolia doltsopa*); compact varieties of *Magnolia grandiflora*, such as 'Little Gem' and Fairy Magnolias®; and *Magnolia laevifolia* (syn. *Michelia yunnanensis*), which reaches 3–4m tall and can be grown as a fragrant hedge or gorgeous potted plant. There's also the less common but still beautiful *Magnolia champaca*, which has light orange flowers during summer and is a great choice for warm climates.

HOW TO GROW:

For in-ground evergreen magnolias:
1. Choose an appropriately sized spot (preferably protected from hot winds) with well-drained soil in full sun to part-shade.
2. Dig a hole twice as wide as the plant's root ball and to the same depth. Enrich the soil dug from the hole with an organic soil improver such as Yates Dynamic Lifter.
3. Remove the plant from the pot, place in the hole and backfill with soil, gently firming down around the root ball.
4. Water well to settle the soil around the roots. Keep the soil moist.

For potted evergreen magnolias:
1. Dwarf varieties of evergreen magnolias are best for pots. Choose a pot at least 40cm wide that has good drainage holes. Position the pot outdoors in a protected, warm, sunny spot.
2. Half-fill the pot with a quality potting mix. Remove the plant from the original pot, position in the new pot and backfill gently with potting mix.
3. Water gently to settle the potting mix around the roots. Keep the potting mix moist.

CLOCKWISE FROM TOP LEFT: *Magnolia grandiflora*; Fairy Magnolia® Blush; *Magnolia champaca*; *Magnolia doltsopa*

GROWING TIPS:

- The popular port wine magnolia is listed separately on page 139.
- Large evergreen magnolias make magnificent shade trees, and their flowers are a favourite with bees.
- Evergreen magnolias can be pruned as required after flowering.
- To promote healthy foliage and lots of flowers, feed regularly from spring to autumn with a potassium-rich plant food such as Yates Thrive Rose & Flower Plant Food.

28

DETAILS:

- LOCATION: Warm temperate to tropical; full sun to part-shade

- FLOWERING TIME: Mid-spring to early summer

- SIZE: 10m tall x 5m wide

HIGHLIGHTS:

- Frangipani-like fragrance

- Ideal for small to medium gardens

- Attracts birds and bees

NATIVE FRANGIPANI

Hymenosporum flavum

Native to coastal rainforest areas in Queensland and northern New South Wales, the native frangipani is an evergreen, upright, narrow tree that usually reaches about 10m tall in a garden setting. Its sweetly scented flowers, reminiscent of exotic frangipanis, start as creamy white and age to a buttery yellow, so during peak flowering the tree will be covered in a lovely mix of cream and yellow flowers. Nectar-feeding birds and bees love feasting on the flowers. Native frangipanis are ideal for growing as leafy shade trees in small- to medium-sized gardens.

HOW TO GROW:

For in-ground native frangipani:
1. Choose a warm frost-free spot with well-drained soil in full sun to part-shade.
2. Dig a hole twice as wide as the plant's root ball and to the same depth. Remove the plant from the pot, place in the hole and backfill with soil, gently firming down around the root ball.
3. Water well to settle the soil around the roots. Keep the soil slightly moist.

For potted native frangipani:
1. Dwarf varieties of native frangipani are best for pots. Choose a pot at least 40cm wide that has good drainage holes. Position the pot outdoors in a warm, sunny, frost-free spot.
2. Half-fill the pot with a quality potting mix. Remove the plant from the original pot, position in the new pot and backfill gently with potting mix.
3. Water gently to settle the potting mix around the roots. Keep the potting mix slightly moist.

GROWING TIPS:

- A dwarf variety called 'Gold Nugget' is available. It grows to about 1m tall and makes a wonderful hedge or potted plant.
- Australian native plants like the native frangipani should be fed with a plant food that's safe for native plants such as Yates Dynamic Lifter.
- Monitor plants for insects such as scale, and diseases such as sooty mould. Consult the pest and disease sections for control recommendations.

29

DETAILS:

- LOCATION: Cool to warm temperate; part-shade
- FLOWERING TIME: Late winter to spring
- SIZE: 0.8–2m tall x 0.5–1m wide

HIGHLIGHTS:

- Australian natives
- Fascinating, small, cup-shaped flowers
- Both species need excellent drainage

BORONIA

Boronia megastigma, B. heterophylla

Brown boronia (*Boronia megastigma*) and red boronia (*B. heterophylla*) are evergreen shrubs native to a small area of south-western Western Australia. They are popular throughout the world as delightfully fragrant plants and cut flowers. Brown boronia has fascinating small flowers that are brown on the outside with a yellow interior, while red boronia has petite bright pink, red or white cup-shaped flowers.

Brown boronia has a (quite well-deserved) reputation for being challenging to grow, but, in the right conditions, it can provide several years of heavenly spicy citrus perfume. Red boronia has more subtly scented flowers (and foliage), but it tends to be slightly easier to grow.

HOW TO GROW:

For in-ground boronia:

1. Choose a wind-protected spot with slightly acidic but very well-drained soil (boronia does not tolerate wet roots) in part-shade (with protection from harsh afternoon sun).
2. Dig a hole twice as wide as the plant's root ball and to the same depth.
3. Carefully remove the plant from the pot (boronia does not like root disturbance), place in the hole and backfill with soil, gently firming down around the root ball.
4. Water well to settle the soil around the roots. Keep the soil moist but not wet.

For potted boronia:

1. Choose a pot at least 30cm wide that has very good drainage holes. Do not use a saucer. Position the pot outdoors in a warm, airy, partly shaded spot.
2. Half-fill the pot with a quality potting mix. Carefully remove the plant from the original pot, position in the new pot and backfill gently with potting mix.
3. Water gently to settle the potting mix around the roots. Keep the potting mix moist but not wet.

Boronia megastigma *Boronia heterophylla*

GROWING TIPS:

- Feed boronia species with a plant food that's safe for Australian native plants, such as Yates Dynamic Lifter.
- Mulch around the base of boronia plants to help keep the soil or potting mix cool and moist, but not wet.
- To promote bushy growth, trim back stems by 30 per cent after flowering.
- When cutting boronia for a vase, choose stems where about half of the flowers have opened.
- Monitor plants for diseases such as root rot. Consult the disease section for control recommendations.

30

DETAILS:

- LOCATION: Temperate to tropical; full sun to part-shade

- FLOWERING TIME: Summer to autumn

- SIZE: 1m tall x 1m wide

HIGHLIGHTS:

- Superb evening fragrance

- Ideal for warm climates

- Beautiful cut flower

BOUVARDIA

Bouvardia longiflora (syn. Bouvardia humboldtii)

Warm-climate gardeners are fortunate to be able to grow this fragrant Mexican native in their garden or potted collection. An evergreen shrub with soft arching stems, bouvardia has superbly scented, tubular, crisp white flowers over many months from summer to autumn. The fragrance peaks at night, so it's best planted where the perfume can drift indoors on warm summer evenings, or position potted bouvardia around outdoor living areas. Bouvardia also makes a gorgeous cut flower and is a popular inclusion in wedding bouquets.

HOW TO GROW:

For in-ground bouvardia:

1. Choose a warm, frost-free, wind-protected spot (bouvardia stems can break easily) with well-drained soil in full sun to part-shade.
2. Dig a hole twice as wide as the plant's root ball and to the same depth. Remove the plant from the pot, place in the hole and backfill with soil, gently firming down around the root ball.
3. Water well to settle the soil around the roots. Keep the soil moist.

For potted bouvardia:

1. Choose a pot at least 30cm wide that has good drainage holes. Position the pot outdoors in a warm, frost-free, wind-protected, sunny or partly shaded spot.
2. Half-fill the pot with a quality potting mix. Remove the plant from the original pot, position in the new pot and backfill gently with potting mix.
3. Water gently to settle the potting mix around the roots. Keep the potting mix moist.

GROWING TIPS:

- To promote healthy foliage and lots of flowers, feed regularly from spring to autumn with a potassium-rich plant food.
- To encourage bushier and tidier growth, prune back stems in late winter after flowering has finished (bouvardia can be trimmed to ground level).
- In cooler areas, potted bouvardia can be brought indoors and kept in a brightly lit room for the winter.
- Monitor plants for insects such as whiteflies and mealybugs. Consult the pest section for control recommendations.
- Some species of bouvardia are not fragrant, so check the plant tag.

31

BUDDLEJA
Buddleja spp.

Buddleja (or buddleia) is also known as butterfly bush, because the flowers are renowned butterfly attractors. A genus of hardy woody shrubs, they are deciduous in cool areas, and tolerant of dry conditions and light frost once established.

Buddlejas have eye-catching long flower spikes over many months that have a deliciously sweet honey fragrance. Their pretty flower colours include white, blue, pale mauve, soft and bright pink, and deep purple. The flowers are enjoyed not only by bees but also by honey-eating birds. You can fill a vase with stems of buddleja flowers, bringing their luscious perfume and gorgeous colour indoors.

DETAILS:
- LOCATION: Cool to sub-tropical; full sun to part-shade
- FLOWERING TIME: Spring to summer
- SIZE: 0.5–5m tall x 0.5–2m wide

HIGHLIGHTS:
- Delightful honey-scented blooms
- Gorgeous range of flower colours
- Attracts butterflies

HOW TO GROW:
For in-ground buddleja:
1. Choose a spot with well-drained soil in full sun to part-shade (flowering will be best in full sun).
2. Dig a hole twice as wide as the plant's root ball and to the same depth. Enrich the soil dug from the hole with an organic soil improver such as Yates Dynamic Lifter.
3. Remove the plant from the pot, place in the hole and backfill with soil, gently firming down around the root ball.
4. Water well to settle the soil around the roots. Once established, buddleja is dry-tolerant but will benefit from being watered thoroughly every 2–3 weeks from spring to autumn.

For potted buddleja:
1. Choose a pot at least 30cm wide that has good drainage holes. Position the pot outdoors in a warm, sunny spot where you will be able to enjoy the fragrance and watch the butterflies.
2. Half-fill the pot with a quality potting mix. Remove the plant from the original pot, position in the new pot and backfill gently with potting mix.
3. Water gently to settle the potting mix around the roots. Keep the potting mix slightly moist.

GROWING TIPS:

- To promote healthy foliage and lots of flowers, feed regularly from spring to mid-autumn with a potassium-rich plant food.
- Dwarf varieties of buddleja, growing to about 50cm tall, are ideal for small gardens and pots.
- In some areas, buddleja has been classified as a weed. To minimise its spread, trim the plant after flowering to prevent seeds from developing.
- To keep buddleja tidy and more compact, and to promote better flowering, hard prune the entire plant back by two-thirds each winter.

32

DETAILS:
- LOCATION: Cool to sub-tropical; part-shade
- FLOWERING TIME: Winter
- SIZE: 1m tall x 1.5m wide

HIGHLIGHTS:
- Winter blooms
- Exquisitely fragrant pink and white flowers
- Needs excellent drainage and dappled shade

DAPHNE
Daphne odora

Daphne's intoxicating scent has often been compared to that of the breakfast cereal Froot Loops®. The clusters of pretty pink and white flowers brighten the gloomy months of winter, and it's hard to resist burying your nose among them to inhale their heady aroma.

Daphne does have a diva reputation, though, heartbreakingly dropping dead if not provided with its ideal conditions. However, excellent drainage, a cool and moist root system as well as dappled shade will provide the best chances of fragrant success.

HOW TO GROW:

For in-ground daphne:
1. Choose a frost-free spot with very well-drained, slightly acidic soil (daphne does not do well in alkaline or heavy clay soil, and does not tolerate wet roots) in full sun (morning sun is preferable) to part-shade.
2. Dig a hole twice as wide as the plant's root ball and to the same depth. Enrich the soil dug from the hole with an organic soil improver such as Yates Dynamic Lifter.
3. Carefully remove the plant from the pot (daphne does not like root disturbance), place in the hole and backfill with soil, gently firming down around the root ball.
4. Water well to settle the soil around the roots. Keep the soil moist but not wet.

For potted daphne:
1. Choose a pot at least 30cm wide that has good drainage holes. Position the pot outdoors in a frost-free, partly shaded spot where you will be able to enjoy the winter fragrance.
2. Half-fill the pot with a quality potting mix. Carefully remove the plant from the original pot, position in the new pot and backfill gently with potting mix.
3. Water gently to settle the potting mix around the roots. Keep the potting mix moist.

GROWING TIPS:

- To promote healthy foliage and lots of flowers, feed every 1–2 weeks with a potassium-rich liquid plant food such as Yates Thrive Rose & Flower Liquid Plant Food.
- Newer varieties such as Daphne 'Perfume Princess'® are more sun-tolerant and have an earlier and longer flowering season.
- Growing daphne in a pot is great option for areas with heavy or poorly drained soil.
- In areas with alkaline soil, apply liquid sulfur to lower the soil pH.
- Mulch around the base of daphne plants to help keep the soil or potting mix cool and moist.
- Monitor plants for insects such as mealybugs and scale, and diseases such as sooty mould. Consult the pest and disease sections for control recommendations.

DETAILS:

- LOCATION: Temperate to tropical; full sun to part-shade
- FLOWERING TIME: Late spring to early autumn
- SIZE: 0.3–2m tall x 0.9–1.5m wide

HIGHLIGHTS:

- Heady summer fragrance
- Versatile range of shrubs and ground covers
- Beautiful potted plants

GARDENIA

Gardenia spp.

With the perfume of gardenias being so heavenly, it's no wonder that they're many people's absolute favourite fragrant plant. Their intoxicating scent has similarities to jasmine and citrus, and a summer evening spent near gardenias is divine.

Gardenias have dark green glossy leaves that are the perfect backdrop for their single or double flowers, which come in snowy white or pale cream, with some turning golden yellow as they age. There are gardenia varieties for almost every space, from low-growing ground covers such as 'Radicans' to tall-growing 'Magnifica' – which can create a beautiful hedge – and medium-sized gardenias that make beautiful potted plants.

HOW TO GROW:

For in-ground gardenia:
1. Choose a frost-free spot with well-drained soil in full sun (with protection from the harsh afternoon sun) to part-shade.
2. Dig a hole twice as wide as the plant's root ball and to the same depth. Enrich the soil dug from the hole with an organic soil improver such as Yates Dynamic Lifter.
3. Remove the plant from the pot, place in the hole and backfill with soil, gently firming down around the root ball.
4. Water well to settle the soil around the roots. Keep the soil moist, and ensure the plant is watered well during summer.

For potted gardenia:
1. Choose a pot at least 30cm wide that has good drainage holes. Position the pot outdoors in a frost-free, warm, sunny spot where you will be able to enjoy the fragrance. In cool areas, position the pot against a protected north-facing wall.
2. Half-fill the pot with a quality potting mix. Remove the plant from the original pot, position in the new pot and backfill gently with potting mix.
3. Water gently to settle the potting mix around the roots. Keep the potting mix moist.

GROWING TIPS:

- Gardenias prefer a slightly acidic soil. In areas with alkaline soil, apply liquid sulfur to lower the soil pH.
- Monitor plants for insects such as aphids and scale, and diseases such as sooty mould. Consult the pest and disease sections for recommendations.
- To promote healthy foliage and lots of flowers, feed regularly from late-winter to mid-autumn with a nitrogen- and potassium-rich plant food like Yates Thrive Rose & Flower Plant Food.
- To maintain a neat shape or reduce the size of the shrub, prune back lightly after flowering has finished.
- Gardenia flower stems can be cut for a (relatively short) vase display. Avoid touching the flowers because this can prematurely discolour them. Individual flowers can also be floated in a shallow bowl of water.

34

DETAILS:

- LOCATION: Temperate to tropical; full sun to part-shade
- FLOWERING TIME: Summer
- SIZE: 1m tall x 1.2m wide

HIGHLIGHTS:

- Purple vanilla-scented flowers
- Cottage-garden favourite
- Attracts butterflies

HELIOTROPE

Heliotropium arborescens

Whether you think the clusters of vivid purple flowers smell like vanilla or warm cherry pie (cherry pie is one of heliotrope's alternative names), this fast-growing but short-lived evergreen shrub can be a wonderfully fragrant inclusion in frost-free gardens. It has interesting, dark purple-green, textured leaves, and the pretty flowers are adored by butterflies. Perfectly at home among other perennials and small shrubs in cottage-garden designs or planted in pots, it provides welcome summer colour and fragrance.

HOW TO GROW:

For in-ground heliotrope:
1. Choose a frost-free spot with well-drained soil in full sun (with protection from the harsh afternoon sun) to part-shade.
2. Dig a hole twice as wide as the plant's root ball and to the same depth. Remove the plant from the pot, place in the hole and backfill with soil, gently firming down around the root ball.
3. Water well to settle the soil around the roots. Keep the soil moist but not wet.

For potted heliotrope:
1. Choose a pot at least 30cm wide that has good drainage holes. Position the pot outdoors in a frost-free, warm, sunny spot (with protection from the harsh afternoon sun) where you will be able to enjoy the fragrance and watch the butterflies.
2. Half-fill the pot with a quality potting mix. Remove the plant from the original pot, position in the new pot and backfill gently with potting mix.
3. Water gently to settle the potting mix around the roots. Keep the potting mix moist but not wet.

GROWING TIPS:

- Heliotrope can be toxic to humans, pets and grazing animals, so plants should be grown in areas inaccessible to children and animals.
- To promote healthy foliage and lots of flowers, feed plants regularly from spring to mid-autumn with a potassium-rich plant food such as Yates Thrive Rose & Flower Plant Food.
- To create new plants, take softwood cuttings of heliotrope in late summer.
- To keep plants tidy and more compact, and to promote better flowering, prune back heliotrope by around one-third after flowering has finished.

35

DETAILS:

- LOCATION: Cool to warm temperate; full sun

- FLOWERING TIME: Late spring to summer

- SIZE: 0.5–1.2m tall x 0.5–1m wide

HIGHLIGHTS:

- Fabulously fragrant cut-flower star

- Attracts bees

- Ideal for pots and border plantings

LAVENDER

Lavandula spp.

Many lavenders are fragrant, but the top perfume prizes go to two types in particular: lavandin (*Lavandula x intermedia*) and some varieties of English lavender (*Lavandula angustifolia*). These lavenders do best in cool to warm temperate climates with dry summers and cool winters, and their grey-green foliage creates a beautiful backdrop for the purple, white or pink flowers that sit atop long thin stems. Lavender looks perfectly at home in cottage-style and mixed flower gardens as well as being a fabulous low hedge or path border, where you can frequently brush past and enjoy its wonderful fragrance.

Lavender also grows very well in a pot, which is an ideal option when the soil is poorly drained. A popular variety of lavandin is the superbly fragrant 'Grosso', which is more tolerant of warm areas and some humidity than English lavender. Lavandin has a higher concentration of camphor and is the best choice for use in potpourri and fragrant crafts. English lavender is the best one for culinary uses, and the varieties 'Munstead' and 'Hidcote' are two fragrant favourites.

HOW TO GROW:

For in-ground lavender:

1. Choose an airy spot with well-drained soil (lavender does not tolerate wet roots) in full sun.
2. Dig a hole twice as wide as the plant's root ball and to the same depth. Enrich the soil dug from the hole with an organic soil improver such as Yates Dynamic Lifter.
3. Remove the plant from the pot, place in the hole and backfill with soil, gently firming down around the root ball.
4. Water well to settle the soil around the roots. Once established, lavender is dry-tolerant but will benefit from being watered thoroughly every 1–2 weeks.

For potted lavender:

1. Choose a pot at least 30cm wide that has good drainage holes. Position the pot outdoors in a warm, sunny spot.
2. Half-fill the pot with a quality potting mix. Remove the plant from the original pot, position in the new pot and backfill gently with potting mix.
3. Water gently to settle the potting mix around the roots. Keep the potting mix slightly moist.

GROWING TIPS:

- Lavender seeds can be sown in spring, while potted plants are best planted from spring to autumn.
- To promote healthy foliage and lots of flowers, feed every 1–2 weeks from spring to mid-autumn with a potassium-rich liquid plant food such as Yates Thrive Rose & Flower Liquid Plant Food.
- To help stop lavender from becoming woody, cut the plants back by two-thirds after flowering has finished.
- When cutting lavender for a vase, choose stems where about half of the flower heads have opened.
- Plant lavender near vegetables and fruit trees that need pollination, because lavender flowers are a magnet for hard-working pollinators such as bees.
- Lavenders prefer a neutral to slightly alkaline soil. In areas with acidic soil, apply liquid lime to raise the soil pH.

36

DETAILS:

- LOCATION: Cold to temperate; full sun to part-shade
- FLOWERING TIME: Spring
- SIZE: 1.5–3m tall x 2–4m wide

HIGHLIGHTS:

- Cool-climate favourite
- Tough deciduous shrub
- Superbly fragrant and pretty flowers

LILAC

Syringa spp.

Lilacs are hardy deciduous shrubs that produce spectacular clusters of fragrant flowers during spring in shades of pink, mauve, light blue, purple, pale yellow or white, some having beautiful multitoned petals. They thrive in cool climates and work wonderfully when grown among evergreen shrubs in cottage-style gardens, because this helps hide lilac's bare winter stems.

It's important to check the plant tag of your chosen lilac – not all are perfumed. Common lilac (*Syringa vulgaris*) is among the most fragrant, with intensely sweet or spicy scented flowers. Growing your own lilacs will reward you with vases full of divine spring colour and fragrance.

HOW TO GROW:

For in-ground lilac:
1. Choose a spot with well-drained soil (lilac does not tolerate wet roots) in full sun to part-shade.
2. Dig a hole twice as wide as the plant's root ball and to the same depth. Enrich the soil dug from the hole with an organic soil improver such as Yates Dynamic Lifter.
3. Remove the plant from the pot (or bag for bare-rooted lilacs), place in the hole and backfill with soil, gently firming down around the root ball.
4. Water well to settle the soil around the roots. Once established, lilac is moderately dry-tolerant but will benefit from being watered thoroughly every 1–2 weeks from spring to autumn.

For potted lilac:
1. Dwarf varieties of lilac are best for pots. Choose a pot at least 50cm wide that has good drainage holes. Position the pot outdoors in a sunny spot.
2. Half-fill the pot with a quality potting mix. Remove the plant from the original pot (or bag for bare-rooted lilacs), position in the new pot and backfill gently with potting mix.
3. Water gently to settle the potting mix around the roots. Keep the potting mix slightly moist from spring to autumn.

GROWING TIPS:

- Lilac can be planted during winter while dormant or during spring.
- To promote healthy foliage and lots of flowers, feed regularly from spring to autumn with a potassium-rich plant food.
- Monitor plants for diseases such as powdery mildew. Consult the disease section for control recommendations.
- To create new plants, take softwood cuttings of lilac after flowering has finished.
- To keep plants tidy, and to promote better flowering, prune back one-third of the oldest and thickest stems each year to ground level.
- Monitor for suckers (shoots) emerging around the plant, which can become invasive. Regularly cut back any unwanted suckers.

37

DETAILS:

- LOCATION: Cool to warm temperate; full sun to part-shade

- FLOWERING TIME: Autumn to winter

- SIZE: 2–3m tall x 1–5m wide

HIGHLIGHTS:

- Clusters of pretty cool-season flowers

- A bygone favourite

- Needs a sheltered spot

LUCULIA

Luculia gratissima

Native to the Himalayas, luculia is an evergreen shrub with large green leaves and clusters of pretty, tubular-shaped, candy pink flowers, which are described as having a tropical fragrance similar to gardenias. Often regarded as a plant of yesteryear (and with a reputation for being a bit temperamental), luculia does best in sheltered cool to warm temperate gardens with well-drained soil. If rhododendrons perform well in your area, luculias are definitely worth adding to your list of fragrant plants to grow.

HOW TO GROW:

For in-ground luculia:
1. Choose a frost-free, wind-protected spot with very well-drained soil (luculia does not tolerate wet roots) in full sun (morning sun is preferable) to part-shade.
2. Dig a hole twice as wide as the plant's root ball and to the same depth. Carefully remove the plant from the pot (luculia does not like root disturbance), place in the hole and backfill with soil, gently firming down around the root ball.
3. Water well to settle the soil around the roots. Keep the soil moist.

For potted luculia:
1. Choose a pot at least 30cm wide that has good drainage holes. Position the pot outdoors in a frost-free, wind-protected, sunny (morning sun is preferable) or partly shaded spot.
2. Half-fill the pot with a quality potting mix. Carefully remove the plant from the original pot, position in the new pot and backfill gently with potting mix.
3. Water gently to settle the potting mix around the roots. Keep the potting mix moist.

GROWING TIPS:

- To promote healthy foliage and lots of flowers, feed regularly with a potassium-rich plant food.
- Mulch around the base of luculia plants to help keep the soil or potting mix cool and moist.
- Luculia prefers a slightly acidic soil.
- If required, luculia can be trimmed back by about one-third after flowering has finished.

38

DETAILS:
- LOCATION: Cool to sub-tropical; full sun to part-shade
- FLOWERING TIME: Spring
- SIZE: 2m tall x 2m wide

HIGHLIGHTS:
- Flowers and foliage smell like citrus
- Hardy dry-tolerant shrub
- Versatile screen, hedge or potted plant

MEXICAN ORANGE BLOSSOM
Choisya ternata

In the same plant family as citrus, and having the common name Mexican orange blossom, there's no surprise that this evergreen shrub has citrusy scented foliage and white flowers. Tolerant of dry conditions and light frost once established, Mexican orange blossom can be grown as a fragrant hedge or screening plant. It is also ideal for a mixed shrub garden or it can be grown in a pot. The species has lush, glossy, mid-green leaves; however, there is also a variety called 'Sundance' with new foliage that is a striking golden yellow.

HOW TO GROW:

For in-ground Mexican orange blossom:
1. Choose a spot with well-drained soil in full sun to part-shade (flowering will be best in full sun).
2. Dig a hole twice as wide as the plant's root ball and to the same depth. Remove the plant from the pot, place in the hole and backfill with soil, gently firming down around the root ball.
3. Water well to settle the soil around the roots. Once established, Mexican orange blossom is moderately dry-tolerant but will benefit from being watered thoroughly every 2–3 weeks from spring to autumn.

For potted Mexican orange blossom:
1. Choose a pot at least 30cm wide that has good drainage holes. Position the pot outdoors in a warm, sunny or partly shaded spot. In cool areas, position the pot against a protected north-facing wall.
2. Half-fill the pot with a quality potting mix. Remove the plant from the original pot, position in the new pot and backfill gently with potting mix.
3. Water gently to settle the potting mix around the roots. Keep the potting mix moist.

GROWING TIPS:

- Protect young plants from frost.
- To promote healthy foliage and lots of flowers, feed regularly from spring to autumn with a potassium-rich plant food.
- For a more formal hedge, or to keep plants more compact, prune back after flowering has finished.
- Monitor plants for insects such as scale. Consult the pest section for control recommendations.

39

DETAILS:

- LOCATION: Cool to warm temperate; full sun to part-shade

- FLOWERING TIME: Spring to summer

- SIZE: 1.5–2.5m tall x 1–2m wide (*Philadelphus mexicanus*); 4m tall x 2.5m wide (*P. coronarius*)

HIGHLIGHTS:

- Sweet orange-blossom fragrance

- Pretty white flowers

- Hardy deciduous or evergreen shrubs

MOCK ORANGE
Philadelphus mexicanus, P. coronarius

In addition to murraya, other popular shrubs known as 'mock orange' are *Philadelphus mexicanus* and *P. coronarius*. They both have white fragrant flowers; evergreen *P. mexicanus* has an orange blossom–like perfume with a hint of rose, and the larger and deciduous *P. coronarius* has a sweet combination of orange blossom and gardenia. They're both hardy plants once established and can be used as informal screening plants or grown among other shrubs.

HOW TO GROW:

For in-ground mock orange:
1. Choose a spot with well-drained soil in full sun to part-shade.
2. Dig a hole twice as wide as the plant's root ball and to the same depth. Remove the plant from the pot, place in the hole and backfill with soil, gently firming down around the root ball.
3. Water well to settle the soil around the roots. Once established, water thoroughly every 2–3 weeks from spring to autumn.

For potted mock orange (*P. mexicanus* is best for growing in pots):
1. Choose a pot at least 30cm wide that has good drainage holes. Position the pot outdoors in a sunny or partly shaded spot. In cool areas, position the pot against a protected north-facing wall until the plant has established.
2. Half-fill the pot with a quality potting mix. Remove the plant from the original pot, position in the new pot and backfill gently with potting mix.
3. Water gently to settle the potting mix around the roots. Keep the potting mix slightly moist (all year for evergreen *P. mexicanus*; from spring to autumn for deciduous *P. coronarius*).

GROWING TIPS:

- To promote healthy foliage and lots of flowers, feed regularly from spring to autumn with a potassium-rich plant food.
- To help keep the plants to a manageable size, prune back stems after flowering has finished. Vigorous *P. mexicanus* stems can be pruned back to knee height after flowering if required.
- Some species of philadelphus are not fragrant, so check the plant tag.
- Once established, evergreen *P. mexicanus* is tolerant of light frosts, while deciduous *P. coronarius* is frost-tolerant.

MURRAYA

Murraya paniculata

Murraya is an evergreen rainforest plant, native to tropical Asia and northern Australia. It's in the same plant family as citrus and is sometimes also known as orange jessamine or mock orange. Murraya is well-known for its dark green leaves and masses of fragrant white flowers, which are reminiscent of orange blossoms. Their perfume is particularly heady at night.

This shrub is widely used to create fast-growing hedges and screens. To promote dense growth, it should be trimmed several times a year, particularly after flowering.

HOW TO GROW:

For in-ground murraya:

1. Choose a frost-free spot with well-drained soil in full sun to part-shade (flowering will be best in full sun).
2. Dig a hole twice as wide as the plant's root ball and to the same depth. Enrich the soil dug from the hole with an organic soil improver such as Yates Dynamic Lifter.
3. Remove the plant from the pot, place in the hole and backfill with soil, gently firming down around the root ball.
4. Water well to settle the soil around the roots. Keep the soil slightly moist.

For potted murraya:

1. Choose a pot at least 30cm wide that has good drainage holes. Position the pot outdoors in a frost-free, warm, sunny spot where you will be able to enjoy the fragrance.
2. Half-fill the pot with a quality potting mix. Remove the plant from the original pot, position in the new pot and backfill gently with potting mix.
3. Water gently to settle the potting mix around the roots. Keep the potting mix moist.

DETAILS:

- LOCATION: Temperate to tropical; full sun to part-shade
- FLOWERING TIME: Spring to summer
- SIZE: 4m tall x 3m wide

HIGHLIGHTS:

- Gorgeous sweet perfume
- Lush green foliage
- Quick-growing hedge, screen or potted plant

GROWING TIPS:

- A dwarf variety called 'Min a Min' has smaller leaves and grows to about 1m tall. It's ideal when shorter hedges are required and is well-suited to topiary.
- In some areas, murraya has been classified as a weed. To minimise its spread, trim the plant after flowering to prevent seed-bearing fruit from developing.
- Murraya usually flowers in spring and summer, but it can also produce a flush of flowers after rain at other times of the year.
- To promote healthy foliage and lots of flowers, feed every 1–2 weeks from spring to autumn with a potassium-rich liquid plant food such as Yates Thrive Rose & Flower Liquid Plant Food.

41

OSMANTHUS

Osmanthus fragrans, O. delavayi

The sweet aroma of ripe apricots or peaches is captured magically in the pale cream flowers of *Osmanthus fragrans*. The flowers are quite inconspicuous, often going unnoticed until their fragrance stops you in your tracks. Also known as fragrant, sweet or tea olive, this is a hardy, slow-growing, evergreen shrub with a tall and upright growth habit that makes it an ideal hedging plant. Its relative, *O. delavayi* – often sold under the names 'Pearly Gates' and 'Heaven Scent' – has larger, white, tubular flowers on a smaller plant with dense dark green foliage. Also beautifully scented, it can be grown as a shorter hedge, among other shrubs in a garden or in a pot.

DETAILS:

- LOCATION: Cool to sub-tropical; full sun to part-shade
- FLOWERING TIME: Winter to spring
- SIZE: 2–4m tall x 1.5–2m wide

HIGHLIGHTS:

- Sweet apricot-like fragrance
- Evergreen shrubs with upright growth
- Slow-growing hedge, mixed-garden or potted plants

HOW TO GROW:

For in-ground osmanthus:
1. Choose a spot with well-drained soil (osmanthus will also tolerate heavier clay soil) in full sun to part-shade.
2. Dig a hole twice as wide as the plant's root ball and to the same depth. Remove the plant from the pot, place in the hole and backfill with soil, gently firming down around the root ball.
3. Water well to settle the soil around the roots. Once established, water thoroughly every 2–3 weeks.

For potted osmanthus:
1. Choose a pot at least 30cm wide that has good drainage holes. Position the pot outdoors in a sunny or partly shaded spot where you will be able to enjoy the fragrance.
2. Half-fill the pot with a quality potting mix. Remove the plant from the original pot, position in the new pot and backfill gently with potting mix.
3. Water gently to settle the potting mix around the roots. Keep the potting mix slightly moist.

GROWING TIPS:

- Protect young plants from frost.
- To promote healthy foliage and lots of flowers, feed regularly with a potassium-rich plant food.
- *Osmanthus fragrans* flowers can be used to flavour tea, jam and desserts.
- To create a formal look or keep the plant to a manageable size, prune back after flowering has finished.

DETAILS:

- LOCATION: Cool to sub-tropical; full sun to part-shade

- FLOWERING TIME: Spring to summer

- SIZE: 3m tall x 2m wide

HIGHLIGHTS:

- Sweet fragrance like bubble gum

- Pretty purple and cream blooms

- Hardy evergreen shrub

PORT WINE MAGNOLIA

Magnolia figo

The port wine magnolia does not have the large goblet-shaped flowers of many other magnolias, but more than makes up for this with its delightful fragrance. The scent of the small purple and cream flowers reminds many people of bubble gum or port wine, although some compare it to bananas, hence its alternative common name: banana shrub. Tolerant of drought and light frosts once established, port wine magnolia is a wonderful evergreen shrub with glossy green leaves. It can be grown among other plants in the garden or on its own in a pot, or it can be planted as a fragrant hedge.

HOW TO GROW:

For in-ground port wine magnolia:
1. Choose a spot with well-drained soil in full sun to part-shade.
2. Dig a hole twice as wide as the plant's root ball and to the same depth. Enrich the soil dug from the hole with an organic soil improver such as Yates Dynamic Lifter.
3. Remove the plant from the pot, place in the hole and backfill with soil, gently firming down around the root ball.
4. Water well to settle the soil around the roots. Once established, water thoroughly every 2–3 weeks.

For potted port wine magnolia:
1. Choose a pot at least 40cm wide that has good drainage holes. Position the pot outdoors in a protected, warm, sunny spot.
2. Half-fill the pot with a quality potting mix. Remove the plant from the original pot, position in the new pot and backfill gently with potting mix.
3. Water gently to settle the potting mix around the roots. Keep the potting mix slightly moist.

GROWING TIPS:

- Protect young plants from frost.
- To promote healthy foliage and lots of flowers, feed regularly with a potassium-rich plant food such as Yates Thrive Rose & Flower Plant Food.
- To keep plants bushy or create a formal hedge, prune to the desired shape after flowering has finished.

43

DETAILS:

- LOCATION: Temperate to tropical; full sun to part-shade

- FLOWERING TIME: Late winter to spring

- SIZE: 1–3m tall x 1–3m wide

HIGHLIGHTS:

- Evening fragrance in late winter and spring

- Pretty pink flowers attract bees and butterflies

- Quick and dense growth

RONDELETIA

Rogiera amoena (syn. Rondeletia amoena), Arachnothryx leucophylla (syn. Rondeletia leucophylla)

Native to Central America, rondeletias are evergreen shrubs that are not as widely grown as they deserve. *Rogiera amoena* has clusters of perfumed salmon-pink flowers, while *Arachnothryx leucophylla* – sometimes called the Panama rose or bush pentas – has vibrant, hot pink flowers.

The fast, dense growth of rondeletias makes them ideal as informal hedges or screening plants, but they are also at home planted among other shrubs. Their nectar-filled flowers are wonderful for attracting birds, bees and butterflies, and rondeletias are perfect for planting near windows and doors where their early evening fragrance can be enjoyed.

HOW TO GROW:

For in-ground rondeletia:

1. Choose a frost-free, wind-protected spot with well-drained soil in full sun to part-shade.
2. Dig a hole twice as wide as the plant's root ball and to the same depth. Remove the plant from the pot, place in the hole and backfill with soil, gently firming down around the root ball.
3. Water well to settle the soil around the roots. Once established, rondeletia is moderately dry-tolerant but will benefit from being watered thoroughly every 2–3 weeks from spring to autumn.

For potted rondeletia:

1. Compact varieties of rondeletia are best for pots. Choose a pot at least 30cm wide that has good drainage holes. Position the pot outdoors in a frost-free sunny or partly shaded spot where you will be able to enjoy the fragrance.
2. Half-fill the pot with a quality potting mix. Remove the plant from the original pot, position in the new pot and backfill gently with potting mix.
3. Water gently to settle the potting mix around the roots. Keep the potting mix slightly moist.

Rogiera amoena

GROWING TIPS:

- To promote healthy foliage and lots of flowers, feed regularly from spring to autumn with a potassium-rich plant food.
- Rondeletia flower stems can be cut for a vase display.
- To create neat hedges, keep plants to a manageable size and encourage dense growth, prune after flowering has finished.
- Rondeletias prefer a slightly acidic soil. In areas with alkaline soil, apply liquid sulfur to lower the soil pH.
- Rondeletias can tolerate coastal conditions.

44

DETAILS:

- LOCATION: Cool to warm temperate; full sun
- FLOWERING TIME: Spring to autumn
- SIZE: 1–1.5m tall x 1m wide; stems of climbers can grow up to 9m long

HIGHLIGHTS:

- Extensive range of beautiful colours
- Fantastic cut flower
- Diverse choice of shrub, climbing and compact roses

ROSES

Rosa spp.

More than 30,000 rose varieties have been developed by plant breeders over the last few centuries, and, thankfully, in recent years there has been a significant focus on breeding for fragrance. The list of fragrant roses is almost endless, from mildly scented varieties to blooms that exude a heady perfume. In that list will be roses with varying notes in their perfumes, such as apricot, apple, pear, citrus, musk, myrrh, vanilla, rose geranium, jasmine and honey, and the overall fragrance can be sweet, spicy, fruity or floral.

There are also different choices when it comes to rose type – from floribunda and hybrid tea roses to climbers and roses that are perfect for pots – flower type and, of course, colour. One of the best ways to pick your favourite variety is to visit a rose garden during spring and give your nose a good workout!

HOW TO GROW:

For in-ground roses:
1. Choose an airy spot with well-drained soil in full sun.
2. Dig a hole twice as wide as the plant's root ball and to the same depth. Enrich the soil dug from the hole with an organic soil improver such as Yates Dynamic Lifter.
3. Remove the plant from the pot (or bag for bare-rooted roses), place in the hole and backfill with soil, gently firming down around the root ball. Ensure that the final soil level sits below the graft union.
4. Water well to settle the soil around the roots. Keep the soil slightly moist from spring to autumn.

For potted roses:
1. Choose a pot at least 40cm wide that has good drainage holes. Position the pot outdoors in a warm, sunny spot where you will be able to enjoy the fragrant flowers.
2. Half-fill the pot with a quality potting mix. Remove the plant from the original pot (or bag for bare-rooted roses), position in the new pot and backfill gently with potting mix. Ensure that the final potting-mix level sits below the graft union.
3. Water gently to settle the potting mix around the roots. Keep the potting mix moist from spring to autumn.

CLOCKWISE FROM TOP LEFT: Papa Meilland; Double Delight; Blue Moon; Boscobel

GROWING TIPS:

- Bare-rooted roses are planted while leafless and dormant in winter. Potted roses can be planted year-round.
- Some of the world's favourite fragrant roses include (but are definitely not limited to) deep red 'Mr Lincoln' and 'Papa Meilland', pink 'Gertrude Jekyll', salmon-pink 'Boscobel', lavender 'Blue Moon' and 'Charles de Gaulle', yellow 'Charles Darwin', and red-and-cream 'Double Delight'.
- To promote healthy foliage and lots of flowers, feed every 1–2 weeks from spring to mid-autumn with a potassium-rich liquid plant food such as Yates Thrive Rose & Flower Liquid Plant Food.
- Regularly trim off spent flowers because this helps keep the rose bush tidy.
- For most shrub-type roses, prune them back by one-third in mid-summer to promote an autumn flower flush and then prune the entire bush back to knee height in winter, also removing any dead or crowded stems.
- Monitor plants for insects such as aphids, caterpillars and scale, and diseases such as black spot and powdery mildew. Consult the pest and disease sections for control recommendations.

DETAILS:

- LOCATION: Cool to sub-tropical; full sun to part-shade
- FLOWERING TIME: Spring
- SIZE: 2–4m tall x 1–2m wide

HIGHLIGHTS:

- Spring fragrance
- Hardy deciduous or evergreen shrubs
- Evergreen species make ideal hedges

VIBURNUMS
Viburnum spp.

There are more than 150 viburnum species, but only a select few have been graced with fragrance. The Korean spice viburnum (*Viburnum carlesii*) is a hardy deciduous shrub with pink buds that open to reveal sweetly scented white flowers in early spring. It's ideal for growing among evergreen shrubs, which will help disguise the viburnum's bare stems in winter.

The Burkwood viburnum (*Viburnum* x *burkwoodii*) is a fast-growing evergreen to semi-deciduous shrub that also has pink buds and white superbly perfumed flowers, followed by red berries. Sweet viburnum (*Viburnum odoratissimum*) is a popular evergreen shrub, often grown as a dense hedge or screening plant, with lush large leaves and clusters of small, white, perfumed flowers in spring.

HOW TO GROW:

For in-ground viburnums:
1. Choose a spot with well-drained soil in full sun to part-shade (flowering will be best in full sun).
2. Dig a hole twice as wide as the plant's root ball and to the same depth. Enrich the soil dug from the hole with an organic soil improver such as Yates Dynamic Lifter.
3. Remove the plant from the pot, place in the hole and backfill with soil, gently firming down around the root ball.
4. Water well to settle the soil around the roots. Keep slightly moist from spring to autumn.

For potted viburnums:
1. Smaller, more compact varieties of viburnum are best for pots. Choose a pot at least 30cm wide that has good drainage holes. Position the pot outdoors in a warm sunny or partly shaded spot where you will be able to enjoy the fragrance.
2. Half-fill the pot with a quality potting mix. Remove the plant from the original pot, position in the new pot and backfill gently with potting mix.
3. Water gently to settle the potting mix around the roots. Keep the potting mix moist. During winter, potted deciduous viburnums need minimal watering.

Burkwood viburnum

GROWING TIPS:

- Deciduous viburnums should be planted in winter. Semi-deciduous and evergreen viburnums can be planted year-round.
- Viburnums are tolerant of moderate frosts once established.
- To promote healthy foliage and lots of flowers, feed regularly from spring to autumn with a potassium-rich plant food.
- 'Anne Russell' is a more compact variety of the Burkwood viburnum, and its flowers have a similar fragrance to daphne.
- For a formal hedge, look for varieties of sweet viburnum that have small dense leaves, such as 'Dense Fence™'.
- To keep viburnums tidy and more compact, prune back after flowering has finished.
- Monitor plants for insects such as scale. Consult the pest section for control recommendations.

DETAILS:

- LOCATION: Cool to sub-tropical; full sun to part-shade

- FLOWERING TIME: Winter

- SIZE: 3m tall x 3m wide

HIGHLIGHTS:

- Sweet winter fragrance

- Fascinating yellow-and-brown flowers

- Hardy deciduous shrub

WINTERSWEET

Chimonanthus praecox

During the gloomiest months of winter, when we're all in need of a boost, wintersweet comes to the rescue! This deciduous shrub produces small, interesting, yellow flowers with a brown centre on its leafless branches in mid-winter. There are differing opinions as to the nature of their fragrance – spicy, a combination of jasmine and jonquils, reminiscent of lemons or honey – however, everyone agrees that the sweet perfume is pure bliss. Apart from its relatively brief winter blooming period, wintersweet is fairly plain, so it should be planted among other shrubs and perennials that are at their best from spring to autumn.

HOW TO GROW:

For in-ground wintersweet:
1. Choose a spot with well-drained soil in full sun to part-shade.
2. Dig a hole twice as wide as the plant's root ball and to the same depth. Remove the plant from the pot (or bag for bare-rooted wintersweet), place in the hole and backfill with soil, gently firming down around the root ball.
3. Water well to settle the soil around the roots. Keep the soil slightly moist while the plant establishes.

For potted wintersweet:
1. Choose a pot at least 30cm wide that has good drainage holes. Position the pot outdoors in a warm sunny or partly shaded spot where the flowers can be enjoyed.
2. Half-fill the pot with a quality potting mix. Remove the plant from the original pot (or bag for bare-rooted wintersweet), position in the new pot and backfill gently with potting mix.
3. Water gently to settle the potting mix around the roots. Keep the potting mix slightly moist from spring to autumn.

GROWING TIPS:

- Wintersweet is best planted during winter.
- To promote healthy foliage and lots of flowers, feed regularly with a potassium-rich plant food.
- If required, prune back the oldest stems after flowering has finished.
- Wintersweet is dry- and frost-tolerant once established.

47

DETAILS:

- LOCATION: Temperate to tropical; full sun to part-shade

- FLOWERING TIME: Spring to summer

- SIZE: 0.6–3m tall x 0.6–1m wide

HIGHLIGHTS:

- Combination of violet, mauve and white flowers

- Foliage is dense and evergreen

- Sweet fragrance

YESTERDAY TODAY TOMORROW

Brunfelsia latifolia

The common name, yesterday today tomorrow, apparently comes from the way the sweetly fragrant flowers on this shrub start out violet and fade to light mauve then white over three days. Its alternative common name, kiss me quick, is also an indication of how rapidly the flowers change colour.

Fortunately, multiple flowers are produced over many weeks, covering the plant in a pretty combination of all three flower colours at once. The dense evergreen foliage makes it a great choice for a hedge or screening plant.

HOW TO GROW:

For in-ground yesterday today tomorrow:

1. Choose a frost-free spot with well-drained soil in full sun to part-shade.
2. Dig a hole twice as wide as the plant's root ball and to the same depth. Enrich the soil dug from the hole with an organic soil improver such as Yates Dynamic Lifter.
3. Remove the plant from the pot, place in the hole and backfill with soil, gently firming down around the root ball.
4. Water well to settle the soil around the roots. Keep the soil slightly moist.

For potted yesterday today tomorrow:

1. Choose a pot at least 30cm wide that has good drainage holes. Position the pot outdoors in a frost-free, warm, sunny spot where you will be able to enjoy the fragrance and admire the multicoloured flower display.
2. Half-fill the pot with a quality potting mix. Remove the plant from the original pot, position in the new pot and backfill gently with potting mix.
3. Water gently to settle the potting mix around the roots. Keep the potting mix moist.

GROWING TIPS:

- Berries and seeds from this plant are toxic to children and pets. Prune lightly after flowering has finished to stop berries forming and keep the plant bushy.
- To promote healthy foliage and lots of flowers, feed every 1–2 weeks from spring to mid-autumn with a potassium-rich liquid plant food such as Yates Thrive Rose & Flower Liquid Plant Food.
- Growing to about 1m tall, dwarf varieties are ideal for small gardens and pots. There is also a variegated variety with attractive cream and green foliage.
- In cool areas, yesterday today tomorrow can be semi-deciduous.

48

LEMON-SCENTED FOLIAGE

Various

What has a lemonier scent than lemons? Plants with lemon-scented foliage! Lemon balm, lemon myrtle, lemon verbena and lemongrass all have deliciously fragrant leaves or stems when crushed, and have the double benefit of being able to be used in lemon-flavoured savoury and sweet dishes. Lemon balm (*Melissa officinalis*) is a fast-growing perennial herb that has sweet lemon-scented leaves. Native to Australian rainforest areas, lemon myrtle (*Backhousia citriodora*) has pretty white flowers and rich lemony foliage. It's a tall tree; however, it can be kept trimmed to shrub size if required. Lemon verbena (*Aloysia citriodora*) is a perennial shrub (semi-deciduous in cooler areas) that can grow up to 3m tall, with intensely aromatic leaves. Lemongrass (*Cymbopogon* spp.) has stems with a citrusy flavour and fragrance, and is a favourite in Asian cooking.

HOW TO GROW:

For in-ground lemon-scented foliage plants:
1. Choose a frost-free spot with well-drained soil in full sun to part-shade.
2. Dig a hole twice as wide as the plant's root ball and to the same depth. Enrich the soil dug from the hole with an organic soil improver such as Yates Dynamic Lifter.
3. Remove the plant from the pot, place in the hole and backfill with soil, gently firming down around the root ball. Lemon balm can also be grown from seed. Scatter the seeds over the bare soil and cover lightly with seed raising mix.
4. Water well to settle the soil around the roots or newly sown seeds. Keep the soil slightly moist.

For potted lemon-scented foliage plants:
1. Choose a pot at least 20cm wide (at least 40cm wide for lemon myrtle) that has good drainage holes. Position the pot outdoors in a frost-free sunny or partly shaded spot where you will be able to brush past or pick the foliage.
2. Half-fill the pot with a quality potting mix. Remove the plant from the original pot, position in the new pot and backfill gently with potting mix. Lemon balm seeds can also be sown into pots. Scatter a few seeds over the potting mix and cover lightly with seed raising mix.
3. Water gently to settle the potting mix around the roots or newly sown seeds. Keep the potting mix slightly moist.

DETAILS:
- LOCATION: Temperate to tropical; full sun to part-shade
- FLOWERING TIME: Summer (lemon balm, lemon myrtle and lemon verbena); not applicable for lemongrass
- SIZE: 30–90cm tall and wide (lemon balm); 3–20m tall x 1–5m wide (lemon myrtle); 3m tall and wide (lemon verbena); 1m tall and wide (lemongrass)

HIGHLIGHTS:
- Lemon-scented bliss
- Use in sweet and savoury recipes
- Grow in the ground or in pots

CLOCKWISE FROM TOP LEFT: lemon balm; lemon myrtle; lemon verbena; lemongrass

GROWING TIPS:

- Additional lemon-scented plants to look out for include lemon thyme, lemon-scented tea tree, lemon mint and lemon basil.
- To promote healthy foliage, feed lemon balm, lemon verbena and lemongrass every week with a soluble plant food, such as Yates Thrive All Purpose Soluble Fertiliser. Feed lemon myrtle regularly with a plant food that's safe for native plants, such as Yates Dynamic Lifter.
- To keep lemon balm, lemon verbena and lemon myrtle more compact and to encourage bushier growth, frequently pick or trim the leaves. Lemongrass stems can be picked once the clump has established.

49

DETAILS:

- LOCATION: Cool to tropical; full sun to part-shade

- FLOWERING TIME: Summer

- SIZE: 0.5–1.3m tall x 0.9m wide

HIGHLIGHTS:

- Intensely scented foliage

- Diverse range of fragrance

- Ideal for pots and shady spots

MINTS

Mentha spp.

Mints are fragrance powerhouses, as their leaves release wonderfully refreshing aromas. There's an enchanting range of mints available, too, from traditional mint and powerful peppermint to mints with the scent of apple, chocolate, citrus, ginger, banana or pineapple.

Delightful when you inhale the fragrance of a crushed bunch of leaves while wandering around the garden or when used in a delicious range of desserts, drinks and savoury recipes, mints are a versatile inclusion in any fragrant garden. Being quite vigorous plants, mints are ideal for growing in pots where their growth can be contained. Mint plants also develop pretty white, pink or mauve flowers in summer, which are a magnet for bees and other beneficial insects.

HOW TO GROW:

For in-ground mints:

1. Choose a spot with well-drained to damp soil in full sun (morning sun is preferable) to part-shade.
2. Dig a hole twice as wide as the plant's root ball and to the same depth. Enrich the soil dug from the hole with an organic soil improver such as Yates Dynamic Lifter.
3. Remove the plant from the pot, place in the hole and backfill with soil, gently firming down around the root ball.
4. Water well to settle the soil around the roots. Keep the soil moist.

For potted mints:

1. Choose a pot at least 20cm wide that has good drainage holes. Mints with a trailing habit can be grown in hanging baskets. Position the pot outdoors in a sunny (morning sun is preferable) or partly shaded spot where you will be able to frequently pick and enjoy the foliage.
2. Half-fill the pot with a quality potting mix. Remove the plant from the original pot, position in the new pot and backfill gently with potting mix.
3. Water gently to settle the potting mix around the roots. Keep the potting mix moist.

GROWING TIPS:

- Mint will tolerate light frosts once established.
- Once the plants are established, feed every 1–2 weeks from spring to autumn with a nitrogen-rich soluble plant food such as Yates Thrive All Purpose Soluble Fertiliser.
- Mint can spread via runners to form large clumps and can become a nuisance. Regularly remove excess growth and runners to keep the plant manageable.
- To create new plants, take 10–15cm-long stem cuttings and place in moist seed raising mix. Keep moist in a protected spot and roots will form over the coming months.
- Potted mint can be grown indoors in a brightly lit spot.
- Monitor plants for insects such as caterpillars and whiteflies. Consult the pest section for control recommendations.

50

DETAILS:

- LOCATION: Cool to warm temperate; full sun to part-shade

- FLOWERING TIME: Summer

- SIZE: 0.5–1.3m tall x 0.9m wide

HIGHLIGHTS:

- Wide range of foliage fragrance options

- Added bonus of pretty flowers

- Tough evergreen perennials

SCENTED PELARGONIUMS

Pelargonium spp.

The foliage of several pelargonium species has the fascinating ability to mimic the fragrance of a diverse range of plants. Often (incorrectly) referred to as scented geraniums, there are scented pelargoniums with leaves that have an unmistakable rose perfume; there are also varieties that smell like lemon, lime, mint, apple, chocolate or candy, and even pelargoniums that have spicy aromas, including nutmeg, ginger or cinnamon.

Grow these hardy evergreen perennials – which also have pretty flowers in pink, purple, red or white – where you can easily grab a handful of leaves to crush and inhale their aroma.

HOW TO GROW:

For in-ground scented pelargoniums:
1. Choose a frost-free spot with well-drained soil (pelargoniums do not tolerate wet roots) in full sun (morning sun is preferable) to part-shade.
2. Dig a hole twice as wide as the plant's root ball and to the same depth. Enrich the soil dug from the hole with an organic soil improver such as Yates Dynamic Lifter.
3. Remove the plant from the pot, place in the hole and backfill with soil, gently firming down around the root ball.
4. Water well to settle the soil around the roots. Keep the soil slightly moist.

For potted scented pelargoniums:
1. Choose a pot or basket at least 20cm wide that has good drainage holes. Scented pelargoniums with a trailing habit can be grown in hanging baskets. Position the pot outdoors in a warm sunny spot where you will be able to frequently brush past or pick and enjoy the foliage.
2. Half-fill the pot with a quality potting mix. Remove the plant from the original pot, position in the new pot and backfill gently with potting mix.
3. Water gently to settle the potting mix around the roots. Keep the potting mix slightly moist.

GROWING TIPS:

- Some species of pelargoniums are not fragrant – check the plant tag for information.
- Once the plants are established, feed every 1–2 weeks from spring to autumn with a soluble plant food such as Yates Thrive All Purpose Soluble Fertiliser.
- To promote more compact growth, regularly prune back stem tips.
- To create new plants, take 10–15cm-long stem cuttings and dip the ends of the cuttings into rooting hormone gel, such as Yates Clonex, before placing in moist seed raising mix. Keep moist in a protected spot and roots will form over the coming months.

FRAGRANT
PLANT CARE

Once you have had the pleasure of choosing some perfumed plants for your garden, there are some key steps to follow regarding planting techniques as well as feeding, watering and protecting plants from common pests and diseases. Here are some simple tips to help maximise your homegrown fragrances.

SOWING AND PLANTING

SOIL PREPARATION

Soil health is a key factor in determining how well your garden will grow, so it's worthwhile dedicating some time to improving the soil before anything is planted. Healthy soil is rich in organic matter, which promotes its moisture- and nutrient-holding capacity, encourages earthworms and beneficial soil microorganisms, and improves soil structure, whether your soil is heavy clay or light sand. Organic matter, in the form of fertilisers and soil improvers such as blood and bone or pelletised chicken manure (for example, Yates Dynamic Lifter), can be mixed into the soil at the base of planting holes, blended into the soil dug from planting holes and used to backfill around the new plant, or mixed into garden beds before planting seeds or seedlings. To improve the soil in established gardens, organic fertilisers can be scattered around the root zone of plants.

Healthy soil also drains well. Most plants do best in well-drained soil; a constantly wet root zone leads to root-rot diseases and poor plant health. How well the soil drains can be easily tested by digging a 30–40cm deep hole, filling it with a bucket of water and watching how quickly it drains away. If there is any water left in the hole after a day, this indicates that the soil is poorly drained. In these areas, it will be helpful to grow plants in 30cm high mounds or raised garden beds that have been filled with quality well-drained soil (bagged garden soil can be purchased from garden centres) and enriched with organic soil improvers. Growing plants in pots is another alternative where the existing soil is poorly drained.

It's also beneficial to know the soil pH, which is a measure of how acidic or alkaline the soil is. The ideal soil pH for most plants is slightly acidic to neutral (pH 6.5–7). When pH levels stray too far above or below neutral, plants can struggle to access nutrients and therefore their health and growth both suffer. Soil pH test kits are readily available from garden centres, as are products that can help lower or raise soil pH if required, such as Yates Soil Acidifier Liquid Sulfur and Yates Hydrangea Pinking Liquid Lime & Dolomite.

HOW TO GROW PLANTS FROM SEEDS

Starting plants from seeds is a wonderfully economical way to grow lots of plants, with each seed packet usually containing dozens or hundreds of seeds. Several fragrant annual and biennial plants – such as alyssum, sweet peas and sweet rocket – do best when they're grown from seed sown direct into the garden bed or pot, rather than being grown in seedling punnets and then being transplanted, so there is no transplant shock.

Perennials such as carnations and wallflowers can also be grown from seed, but it's best to start them in trays or punnets of seed raising mix, and then transplant the seedlings into their final home. This method is also more cost-effective than buying seedlings from nurseries or garden centres. It's best to use specialised seed raising mix, rather than normal potting mix, when growing your own seedlings, because it has a finer grade that allows much better contact (and ultimate success) with the seeds.

Before sowing seeds directly into garden beds or pots, check the information on the seed packet. It will include specific details on the correct season to sow, how deep to sow the seeds, watering requirements and early-care tips. Here are the basic seed-sowing steps:

- Make a small hole or shallow furrow in the soil, potting mix or seed raising mix at the required depth for the seed.
- Place one or more seeds into each hole, or sprinkle seeds along the furrow.
- Cover the seeds with soil, potting mix or seed raising mix, and keep moist throughout the germination period. Some seeds, such as those of sweet peas, don't like to be kept too moist during this phase.
- It's a good idea to place a tag or marker to indicate where and what seeds have been sown and the date.
- Some seeds germinate rapidly, whereas others can take several weeks. Seed packets will indicate the average germination time.
- If too many seedlings emerge from the one hole or furrow, the smallest plants can be removed, leaving enough room for the remaining seedlings to grow. Sometimes, you can carefully save and transplant these small excess seedlings elsewhere.
- If you've grown your own seedlings in trays or punnets, transplant them into their final garden or pot home when they're large enough to handle.

HOW TO PLANT SEEDLINGS

Whether you've grown your own seedlings, or bought seedlings from your local garden centre, dig a small hole in your garden bed or pot that is large enough to fit the entire root ball of the seedling. All the seedling's roots need to be covered with soil or potting mix, but with most plants it's best not to go any deeper. It's important that the roots are covered but not the stem.

Seedlings are quite delicate, so transplant them very carefully to minimise root damage.

Using a gentle hose setting or a watering-can rose, thoroughly water the seedlings after they're transplanted, to settle the soil or potting mix around the roots. Applying a diluted seaweed solution at this time can help reduce transplant shock and promote early root growth.

HOW TO PLANT BULBS

Bulbs are packed with the hidden promise of future flowers and fragrance. Spring-flowering bulbs are planted during autumn, while summer- and autumn-flowering bulbs are planted in spring or summer, depending on the type of bulb.

Bulbs should be planted in well-drained soil or potting mix, and to the depth indicated on the bulb pack. For example, hyacinths should be planted 12cm deep, and belladonna lily should be planted with the top of the bulb just above the soil surface.

The bulb label should also indicate how far apart to space the bulbs, with bulbs looking their most attractive when planted in groups of three or more. Bulbs growing in pots can be planted more closely together than in-ground bulbs. It's also important to plant the bulbs the right way up! For most bulbs, plant them with the pointy end up.

Lily of the valley

HOW TO PLANT BARE-ROOTED PLANTS

Deciduous plants, such as roses and lilacs, are commonly available 'bare-rooted' during winter while they are leafless and dormant. Planting deciduous plants during winter is ideal, as they suffer minimal transplant shock and will be ready to start growing as soon as the weather warms in spring. The root systems of bare-rooted plants are usually surrounded by a plastic bag filled with moist potting mix or sawdust. It's crucial not to let the roots dry out. When you get the plant home, soak the root ball in a bucket of diluted seaweed solution for a few hours. This keeps the roots moist, and the seaweed will also promote new root growth.

For in-ground plants, dig a hole twice as wide as the root system and to the same depth. Enrich the soil dug from the hole with an organic soil improver such as Yates Dynamic Lifter. At the base of the hole, create a pyramid-shaped mound of soil. Carefully untangle the roots and spread them over the top of your mound of soil in the hole. Gently backfill around the roots with the enriched soil, ensuring the final level of soil is the same as the original level of soil or potting mix on the plant's stem. If the plant is grafted, ensure the graft union (bump on the stem) is sitting at least 5cm above the soil. Water well to settle the soil around the roots.

For potted plants, half-fill the pot with a quality potting mix and create a pyramid-shaped mound of potting mix in the centre of the pot. Carefully untangle the roots and spread them over the top of your mound of potting mix in the pot. Gently backfill around the roots with potting mix, ensuring the final level of potting mix is the same as the original level of soil or potting mix on the plant's stem. If the plant is grafted, ensure the graft union is sitting at least 5cm above the potting mix. Water well to settle the potting mix around the roots.

If your plant needs to be supported with a stake or trellis, it's best to insert it into the ground or pot at the time of planting, to avoid damaging the roots later.

TOP: Bare-rooted rose

BOTTOM: Planting a bare-rooted rose

HOW TO PLANT TREES, SHRUBS AND CLIMBERS

Most evergreen potted trees, shrubs and climbers bought from your local garden centre or via mail order can be planted at any time of the year; however, the milder conditions in spring and early autumn are the best times for planting. Frost-sensitive plants growing in cool climates should be planted during spring, giving them many months to establish prior to the onset of winter. To help reduce transplant shock, thoroughly water your new plant a few hours prior to planting.

To plant in-ground trees, shrubs and climbers, dig a hole twice as wide as the plant's root ball and to the same depth. Enrich the soil dug from the hole with an organic soil improver such as Yates Dynamic Lifter. Remove the plant from the pot (it can help to squeeze the sides of the pot first to loosen the roots and potting mix). If the roots are compacted or circling around the root ball, it's beneficial to tease out some of the roots; this will encourage the roots to grow out into the surrounding soil. Place the root ball in the hole and backfill around the roots with the enriched soil. Ensure that the final level of soil is the same as the original level of potting mix on the plant's stem. Water well to settle the soil around the roots. Applying a diluted seaweed solution around the root zone of the new plant can help reduce transplant shock and promote root growth.

When growing plants in pots, half-fill the pot with a quality potting mix. Remove the plant from the original pot, gently tease out any compacted roots and place the root ball in the new pot. Backfill gently around the roots with potting mix, ensuring the final level of potting mix is the same as the original level of potting mix on the plant's stem. Water gently to settle the potting mix around the roots.

For climbing plants or plants requiring a support, position them next to an existing fence, pergola or trellis. Ideally, insert a new support, such as a tripod or post, into the soil or potting mix at the time of planting, because this avoids damaging the root system later.

It's important to regularly water new in-ground and potted plants for several months while they're establishing.

GROWING FRAGRANT PLANTS IN POTS

Not having a front- or backyard garden, or having limited space, doesn't mean you need to miss out on growing your own perfumed plants, because there is a wonderful range of pot-perfect options. Potted plants also introduce fantastic flexibility into your gardening, because pots can be used when there's no soil to garden in, or the soil you have is of poor quality. Pots can also be moved around your outdoor spaces to make the most of microclimates or when plants are looking and smelling their best, or pots can be shuffled between houses when you're on the move.

What follows is some simple information about how to get the best out of potted fragrant plants.

POTTING MIX

It's definitely worth investing in good-quality potting mix. Don't be tempted to dig up soil from your garden and use it instead, because this is one of the quickest ways to kill your new plant! Garden soil typically does not have the correct structure and drainage to be able to support healthy potted plant growth.

Potting mixes are typically blends of composted pine bark, sand and plant fertilisers, and some contain additives such as wetting agents, water-absorbent crystals and beneficial microorganisms. There is a wide range of different types and grades of potting mixes available; however, for most fragrant plants, a premium-grade potting mix such as Yates Premium Potting Mix is ideal.

Some potting mixes contain slow-release fertilisers that will gradually feed the plant during its early months. Check the bag of your chosen potting mix for information on when to start fertilising your new plants.

USING POTTING MIX SAFELY

Potting mix contains microorganisms and particles that can be harmful if they are inhaled or come into contact with skin and eyes, particularly for people with allergies or compromised immune systems. When handling potting mix, wear gloves and a dust mask, and wash your hands thoroughly afterwards. Potting-mix bags will contain information on how to handle the mix safely.

POTTING MIX RE-USE TIP

When growing annual or biennial flowers in pots, once the plants have reached the end of their life cycle, you don't need to throw away the potting mix. It can be refreshed by blending in some fresh potting mix or adding organic matter such as a fine grade of coconut fibre (also known as coir peat) and a handful of composted pelletised manure (which also provides organic nutrients to feed plants). To reinvigorate old potting mix, tip it into a large plastic container, add the fresh ingredients and give it a thorough stir. Then it is ready to use for your next potted fragrant beauty.

HOW TO CHOOSE A POT

There is a wonderfully diverse range of pots to tempt you, ranging from plain black and decorative plastic pots to colourful glazed ceramic pots, hanging baskets, self-watering pots, rustic-looking terracotta pots, lightweight fibreglass and composite pots, and recycled and repurposed containers. You can coordinate your pots with your garden style and outdoor decor. Whatever your budget, there will be a pot to suit.

Each of the plant profiles in this book provides an indication of the size of pot that you'll need. Small pots (<20cm diameter) can't hold as much potting mix as larger pots, so they can require a lot of maintenance; they will exhaust their supply of nutrients and moisture much faster than larger pots. They'll also heat up more rapidly, which can be stressful for a plant's root system and general health. Medium-sized pots (30–40cm diameter) won't dry out quite as quickly and can be easier to look after. Bear this in mind when choosing your pots – particularly if watering several times a day during summer is not possible, or if the pots are going to be in a hot and exposed location.

Large pots (>50cm diameter) can hold the most moisture and nutrients, so are easier to maintain. Larger plants and trees require a larger pot; however, unless your plant is a fast grower, it's best not to put a small young plant into a pot that is significantly bigger than the original pot the plant has come in. A small plant growing in a big pot often results in an unhealthy environment around the roots, and plant health can suffer. Where you can, it's better to gradually increase the size of the pot as the plant grows. Also consider the size of your plant in relation to the dimensions of the pot. For example, a tall shrub in a small or shallow pot will look strange and is prone to tipping over. Potted plants will look at home when the size of the pot matches the size of the plant.

If you have a large pot or barrel you'd like to use, but want to grow small plants, then try planting multiple plants in the one pot. You can mass plant the one type of plant, such as spring-flowering bulbs like hyacinths, or choose a mix of compact plants that prefer the same amount of sunshine and water as each other. These mixed plants could flower at the same time or be a combination of plants (all fragrant or a blend of fragrant and non-fragrant plants) that flower at different times throughout the year, which helps to extend the floral show.

A good choice for beginner gardeners, when regular watering may not be possible, or for particularly thirsty plants, is a self-watering pot. They have a water reservoir in the base, which plants can draw upon over several days or weeks.

Adequate drainage holes in pots are crucial because too much water retained in a pot can lead to root rot, which can quickly kill a plant. When it comes to pots with saucers, unless the weather is going to be hot or you're heading away for a few days, don't allow water to sit in the saucer for more than a day or so. It can cause a permanently soggy zone of potting mix at the base of the pot and lead to root rot.

Don't forget hanging baskets and vertical gardens, too, which are wonderful ways to make the most of your space. Plants that can cascade, such as sweet peas, are ideal for hanging baskets, while trailing plants such as mint are perfect for vertical gardens.

FEEDING FRAGRANT PLANTS

Well-fed plants are healthier and better able to resist pests and diseases, and they will reward you with a much better display of fragrant flowers and foliage. This is particularly important for potted plants, which deplete their supply of nutrients much faster than in-ground plants. So, regular fertilising is an important part of growing a flourishing fragrant garden.

Different types of fertilisers are suitable for feeding in-garden and potted plants. These include liquids, soluble plant foods, pellets, prills and granules, and they can be made from synthetic ingredients, organic materials or a combination of both.

- **Liquid fertilisers** – usually containing fast-acting nutrients, liquid plant foods are mixed with water then applied over the foliage and soil or potting mix using a watering can. Liquid fertilisers provide plants with an instant feed and have to be reapplied on a regular basis, usually every 1–2 weeks.
- **Soluble fertilisers** – similar to liquid fertilisers, they contain fast-acting nutrients but consist of a blend of powdered fertilisers that are dissolved in water before use. Soluble fertilisers need to be reapplied every 1–2 weeks.
- **Pelletised fertilisers** – often containing organic ingredients such as manure, pelletised fertilisers release nutrients slowly to the plant over several weeks or months as they break down. They also add organic matter to the soil or potting mix, and encourage beneficial soil microorganisms. Some pelletised manures are boosted with fast-acting nutrients.
- **Prilled fertilisers** – these are small granules of compressed fertiliser that may be coated to slow down the release of nutrients (they're often referred to as controlled-release fertilisers). Sprinkled over the surface of the soil or potting mix, they release nutrients to the plant slowly over many weeks or months.
- **Granular fertilisers** – these granules contain a concentrated blend of nutrients that are best suited to garden beds; however, check the product label to see whether they're also suitable for feeding potted plants.

Plants require three main nutrients for healthy growth: nitrogen (N), which promotes green leaf and stem growth; phosphorus (P), which encourages strong root development; and potassium (K), which helps flowering, fruiting and healthy plant growth. A fertiliser that contains these three nutrients is called a 'complete' plant food. It's important to feed plants with complete plant foods to ensure they receive all the nutrients they require for healthy growth.

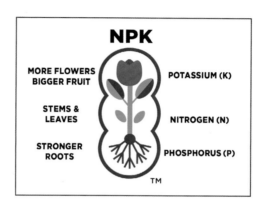

Different plants do best with specially developed complete plant foods, which contain the right balance of nitrogen, phosphorus and potassium to promote growth and development of the part of the plant you want to enjoy. For example, leafy fragrant plants such as mint and lemon balm should be fed with a plant food that contains lots of nitrogen, which is the nutrient that promotes healthy green leaf growth. Nitrogen-rich Yates Thrive All Purpose Soluble Fertiliser is ideal for feeding leafy plants. Flowering plants should be fed with a potassium-rich fertiliser, because potassium is an important nutrient for encouraging more flowers. Yates Thrive Rose & Flower fertilisers are boosted with additional potassium and are the best choice for feeding flowering plants.

When plants are in an active period of foliage growth or are flowering, they need feeding to enable them to grow and flower to their full potential. This includes plants that are growing new foliage or flowering during winter.

When growing bulbs, don't cut off yellowing bulb foliage at the end of the flowering season. It's important to let the foliage die down naturally, because this allows the bulbs to absorb as much sunshine (and thus energy) as possible for the next year. It's also important to keep feeding bulbs regularly until the foliage dies down, allowing the plants to store as many nutrients as possible for future foliage and flowers.

HOW TO WATER

A key part of promoting healthy plant growth is providing plants with enough moisture. The plant information pages in this book provide general watering guidelines for each plant. Most plants prefer to be kept slightly moist, particularly during the warmest months of the year, and watering can be reduced during winter when conditions are cooler and plant growth slows. Some plants prefer a drier environment, while others like it moister, so it's good to know how thirsty your chosen plants are. It's also important to note that plants growing in pots dry out much faster than in-ground plants, so monitoring the moisture levels in your potted plant collection is vital. A simple way to check moisture levels in soil and potting mix is with your finger. Insert your finger into the top few centimetres of soil or potting mix, and you'll be able to feel whether it's still moist and you can leave rewatering for another few days, or whether it feels dry and dusty and needs to be watered.

When planting new plants, it's important to water them thoroughly immediately after planting, because this helps to settle the soil or potting mix around the roots and reduce any large air pockets. For newly transplanted plants, regular watering for at least the first 3 months is essential, because the root ball will still only be relatively small (the size of the original pot) until the roots begin to grow into the surrounding soil or potting mix. When planting new plants in spring or summer, it's best to keep the plants well-watered until the cooler weather arrives in autumn, because hot and dry summer weather can be challenging for new plants.

Using the right watering technique will also be beneficial to plant health and survival. When plants are established, it's best to water thoroughly and deeply, once or twice a week, rather than applying small amounts of water each day. Deep watering moves moisture down into the lower layers of soil, which encourages roots to grow deeper where they can access more moisture and a cooler root zone. This larger root zone can help make plants more resilient during dry weather. When plants are watered shallowly and moisture stays in the upper layers of soil, the roots will be concentrated near the soil surface and be more prone to heat stress during drought conditions. So, it benefits plants if you devote more time to watering on each occasion, but to water less often.

LEFT: Water repellent potting mix

BELOW: Micro irrigation system

The right watering technique can also assist with reducing plant diseases. Spores can be splashed up onto the foliage from the soil or potting mix, so watering the surface of the soil or potting mix directly and gently can help minimise this. For many plants, damp foliage – particularly overnight – can increase the risk of disease. Watering in the morning allows foliage to dry out during the day.

For plants growing in pots, saucers can catch excess water; however, unless the weather is predicted to be very warm, don't leave water in pot saucers for more than a day or so. This creates a constantly soggy layer of potting mix at the bottom of the pot, which can lead to roots rotting and the potting mix anaerobically decomposing. Self-watering pots, hanging baskets and troughs are specially designed to have a water-holding reservoir in the base, and plants can draw on this water over several days as they need it. Self-watering pots are a great option for gardeners who may not be able to (or forget to!) water their potted plants as often as required, or need the flexibility to be able to leave their plants for a few days at a time.

An irrigation system is useful for large garden areas or collections of potted plants. Drip and micro-sprinkler systems are efficient ways to water your plants, because they regularly deliver water over the root zone. A timer can be included in the system, so your plants will still be watered when you're too busy or you go away on holidays.

Particularly during dry weather, soil and potting mix can become water repellent (hydrophobic). Moisture no longer moves evenly or effectively down into the root zone, and water can pool on the surface. In potted plants, the potting mix can also dry and shrink away from the pot wall; when the plant is watered, the liquid may seep down between the pot wall and the edge of the potting mix and not penetrate into the root ball of the plant, even though water flows out from the bottom of the pot. You can help to re-wet soil and potting mix by applying a soil-wetting agent such as Yates Waterwise Soil Wetter. Soil-wetting agents help break down the waxy, water-repellent layer and enable moisture to move more successfully down into the root zone. Wetting agents can be reapplied several times a year on gardens and potted plants.

Watering can often be decreased over the cooler months, as plant growth slows and air temperatures drop. However, plants that actively grow and flower during winter will still need regular moisture to thrive. Continue to monitor soil and potting mix moisture levels during winter to determine when you need to rewater.

PESTS

Pests can affect plant foliage, stems and flowers, leading to plants becoming unhealthy and the reduction or loss of a much-anticipated floral show. Pests can be kept under control once you know the early symptoms to look for. First, work out which pest you're dealing with and then choose the appropriate control method.

Here are some of the most common pests that occur on flowering plants:

- **Aphids** – these small insects can breed very rapidly and feed on plant sap. Aphids are about 2mm long and can be black, grey, yellow, green or brown. They are particularly attracted to soft new growth, but can also infest older leaves and stems as well as attack other parts of plants, including flower buds and petals. Affected leaves can curl and yellow, flowers can distort, petals can become marked and plant health can suffer. Aphids can transmit damaging plant viruses from one plant to another. In addition, aphids excrete a sweet sticky substance called honeydew, which attracts ants. It also encourages a fungal disease called sooty mould, which appears as a dark grey or black ash-like coating over leaves and stems.

- **Caterpillars** – these chewing insects make holes in leaves, stems, flower buds and petals. Caterpillars come in varying colours and textures, from brown, green, striped or spotted to smooth or hairy. They are often camouflage experts and hard to find; their damage or droppings are the first things that are noticed.

- **Citrus leaf miner** – curled and twisted citrus leaves with silvery trails are caused by the larvae of the citrus leaf miner moth tunnelling into new foliage. It's a common pest for Australian citrus growers that needs to be prevented by spraying new foliage with an oil-based spray.

- **Snails and slugs** – silvery trails, holes in leaves and flowers, damaged stems and completely destroyed seedlings are all signs that snails and slugs are in your garden. They are more common when conditions are cool and moist; however, they can be present year-round with sufficient moisture, coming out at dusk to feed on both in-ground and potted plants.

- **Mealybugs** – these sap-sucking insects can infest trees, shrubs and climbers. Mealybugs are about 3mm long and are covered in a white furry or hairy coating. They are often found on the lower stems of plants, hiding among leaf bases and on the underside of leaves, but they can attack all parts of plants. Mealybugs deplete plants of valuable nutrients and sugars, and adversely affect plant health. They excrete a sweet sticky substance called honeydew, which attracts ants. It also encourages a fungal disease called sooty mould.

CLOCKWISE FROM TOP LEFT: Aphids, caterpillar, mealybugs and snail

- **Spider mites** – sometimes called two-spotted mites, spider mites are tiny sap-sucking pests. Less than 1mm long, these are difficult to see with the naked eye. The first noticeable symptom is usually yellowing or mottled foliage, and when spider-mite colonies increase, they will form spidery webbing between leaves and over flowers. Spider mites like hot dry weather, so are more common during summer. Mite infestations damage plant health and can cause plants to die if left untreated.

- **Scale** – these are sap-feeding insects that hide under a hard, soft or furry waxy coating that can be white, grey, brown or black. Commonly seen on shrubs and trees, they're 3–5mm long and can attack leaves, stems and branches. Scale insects on leaves can cause a corresponding yellow spot on the opposite leaf surface, and plant growth can slow down as the insects remove important sugars and nutrients from the plant. They also produce honeydew, which attracts ants and encourages the fungal disease called sooty mould.

- **Whiteflies** – these white flying insects are 1–2mm long. They breed rapidly to create large colonies and will often fly up in a cloud when disturbed. They suck the sap from plants, causing plant health to decline, and secrete honeydew that encourages the fungal disease called sooty mould.

- **Thrips** – tiny insects just 0.5–1.5mm long, thrips feed on plant juices and can cause leaves to distort and become mottled and silvery. Some thrips feed specifically on flowers, causing petals to develop brown spots, particularly on light-coloured flowers. Thrips can also transmit damaging plant viruses.

- **Bronze orange bugs** – sometimes referred to as stink bugs, bronze orange bugs are an Australian sap-feeding citrus pest that significantly damage young new leaves and stems, as well as flower and fruit stalks.

- **Possums** – these agile climbers can eat leaves, stems and flower buds in even the highest of places. Wire mesh or bird netting can help deter possums, as can possum-deterrent sprays.

- **Birds** – our feathered friends will enjoy visiting your flower-filled garden; however, some birds can scratch up young seedlings. Bird netting or wire mesh can be used to protect plants when they're young.

- **Earwigs** – these small insects have pincers at the end of their abdomen and can chew into seedlings, leaves and flowers.

CLOCKWISE FROM
TOP LEFT: Spider mites,
whiteflies, earwig and thrips

HOW TO CONTROL PESTS

A small number of pests can still inflict damage on your plants, so the sooner you spot and act upon a pest infestation, the better. A few pests can be gently scraped away, picked off, squished or sometimes given a firm squirt with the hose.

Insect-eating birds and predatory insects can help keep pest numbers down. Here are some beneficial garden visitors:

- **Ladybirds** – most types of ladybirds are predatory and will eat small insect pests such as aphids, mealybugs and scale. There are also some ladybirds that feed on the disease powdery mildew.
- **Praying mantises** – there are lots of different praying mantises, and they eat pest insects such as aphids and caterpillars.
- **Parasitic wasps** – these tiny wasps control caterpillars by laying their eggs in various types of caterpillars or the eggs from which caterpillars hatch.
- **Lacewings** – the most common lacewings are about 1cm long and are green or brown with delicate transparent wings. Lacewings eat aphids and other small soft insects.
- **Hoverflies** – juvenile hoverflies feed on aphids and thrips, while the adults – which are often striped black and yellow – are wonderful pollinators.
- **Predatory mites** – as the name suggests, predatory mites feed on pest mites. Different predatory mites control different pest mites.
- **Insectivorous birds** – small birds often devour insect pests.

Encourage predatory insects to visit your garden by growing a variety of plants that flower at different times throughout the year, because these plants produce pollen that provides the insects with an additional source of food. Flowers will also entice pollinating insects into your garden and outdoor spaces, which is vital if you're growing your own fruit and vegetables. Check your plants regularly for signs of predatory insects, and avoid spraying plants with insecticides if predators are present. Small insect-eating birds prefer gardens that have dense plants to hide in, so growing leafy and woody shrubs can help create an enticing habitat for them.

CLOCKWISE FROM TOP LEFT: Ladybird, lacewing, and hoverfly

For large infestations of pests, here are some products that can help control the pests and protect your plants.

PEST	SOLUTION	ORGANIC SOLUTION
Aphids Spider mites Whiteflies	Yates Rose Gun Yates Rose Shield (Aust. only) Yates Super Shield (NZ only) Yates Mavrik	Yates Nature's Way Vegie & Herb Spray (Natrasoap) (Aust. only) Yates Nature's Way Citrus & Ornamental Spray (Aust. only) Yates Nature's Way Natrasoap Vegie Insect Gun (NZ only) Yates Nature's Way Organic Citrus, Vegie & Ornamental Spray (NZ only)
Mealybugs	Yates Scale Gun (Aust. only) Yates Nature's Way Fruit & Vegie Gun (NZ only)	Yates Nature's Way Citrus & Ornamental Spray (Aust. only) Yates Nature's Way Organic Citrus, Vegie & Ornamental Spray (NZ only) Yates Conqueror Spraying Oil (NZ only)
Thrips	Yates Rose Gun Yates Rose Shield (Aust. only) Yates Super Shield (NZ only) Yates Mavrik	Yates Nature's Way Vegie & Herb Spray (Natrasoap) (Aust. only) Yates Nature's Way Citrus & Ornamental Spray (Aust. only) Yates Nature's Way Organic Citrus, Vegie & Ornamental Spray (NZ only)
Scale	Yates Scale Gun (Aust. only) Yates PestOil (Aust. only)	Yates Nature's Way Citrus & Ornamental Spray (Aust. only) Yates Conqueror Spraying Oil (NZ only)
Citrus leaf miners (Australia) Bronze orange bugs on citrus (Australia)	Yates Nature's Way Citrus & Ornamental Spray (Aust. only) Yates PestOil (Aust. only) for citrus leaf miner	Yates Nature's Way Citrus & Ornamental Spray (Aust. only)

PEST	SOLUTION	ORGANIC SOLUTION
Caterpillars	Yates Rose Gun Yates Rose Shield (Aust. only) Yates Super Shield (NZ only) Yates Nature's Way Natural Insect Spray Pyrethrum (NZ only) Yates Success Ultra Insect Control Yates Mavrik	Yates Nature's Way Citrus & Ornamental Spray (Aust. only) Yates Nature's Way Caterpillar Killer Dipel (Aust. only) Yates Nature's Way Organic Citrus, Vegie & Ornamental Spray (NZ only)
Snails and slugs	Yates Blitzem Snail & Slug Pellets Yates Snail & Slug Bait (Aust. only)	
Possums	Yates Possum Repellent (Aust. only)	
Earwigs	Yates Pyrethrum Insect Pest Gun (Aust. only) Yates Nature's Way Natural Insect Spray Pyrethrum (NZ only)	Yates Nature's Way Citrus & Ornamental Spray (Aust. only) Yates Nature's Way Organic Citrus, Vegie & Ornamental Spray (NZ only)

These tables are a general guide only. It's important to check product labels before spraying. Some products are not registered to control all pests on all plants, particularly edible plants.

Ensure that plants are not suffering from moisture stress when they're sprayed, because dehydrated plant foliage can be damaged. It's important to spray both sides of the leaves, because many insects will hide underneath leaves and are only controlled when the spray physically touches them. Always use sprays as per the use and safety directions on the label.

DISEASES

Flowering plants can be affected by several common diseases, which are caused by fungal or bacterial organisms. The most common diseases that affect flowering plants include:

- **Black spot** – a fungal disease of roses, it causes feathery-margined black spots and yellowing on leaves. It's common during damp and humid conditions.

- **Blight** – this encompasses fungal diseases that cause leaves and stems to brown, flowers to discolour and drop, and – in serious cases – plants to wilt and die. Blight can also cause seedlings to die (called damping off). Lilacs, roses and geraniums are susceptible to blight. Cool moist weather promotes blight problems.

- **Botrytis** – this name covers a range of fungal diseases that cause varying symptoms, including the rotting of peony stems and flowers, and grey mould covering rose buds and blooms. Botrytis is more common during humid, wet and cool weather.

- **Leaf spots** – brown or black spots develop into holes and spread to cover large areas of the leaves.

- **Downy mildew** – this disease appears as tufty grey or discoloured patches underneath leaves, with corresponding yellow or dark markings on the upper surface of the leaves. Downy mildew can result in dying or dead spots on foliage. Rose downy mildew (specific to roses) causes leaves to develop yellow spots, which change to purple, red or black, and the plant can defoliate.

- **Powdery mildew** – a fungal disease that favours warm and humid conditions, it appears as spots of white or grey ash over leaves, stems and flower buds, which can eventually cover large areas of the plant. Affected leaves can turn yellow and develop brown or dead patches.

- **Root rot** – plants with root rot will often start to wilt, due to their inability to absorb sufficient moisture. Wilting foliage caused by root rot may be confused with dehydrated plants due to underwatering, so it's important to check soil moisture levels.

- **Rust** – orange, yellow or reddish pustules develop on leaves or stems and have a corresponding yellow spot on the other side of the leaves.

- **Sooty mould** – this disease looks like black ash covering leaves and stems. Sooty mould grows on the sweet and sticky honeydew that is excreted by sap-sucking insects, such as aphids, scale and mealybugs. Once the insects are controlled, the sooty mould will disappear.

CLOCKWISE FROM TOP LEFT: Powdery mildew, sooty mould, botrytis and rust

HOW TO CONTROL DISEASES

Well-fed plants growing in their ideal climate and garden location will be less susceptible to disease. For example, plants that like growing in a warm, airy, full-sun position will be at a greater risk of disease when grown in a cool, humid, shady spot. So whenever possible, match your plant with its preferred environment, and it will be much healthier and more resistant to disease.

Disease incidence can also be reduced through correct watering techniques. Disease spores can be splashed up from the soil or potting mix and onto the foliage, but careful and gentle watering around the base of the plant will minimise this. Damp foliage, particularly overnight, can also increase the risk of disease. Watering in the morning allows leaves to dry out during the day, reducing the ability of the diseases to survive. As soon as any disease symptoms are noticed, the affected leaf or a few leaves can be removed to help prevent the spread to healthy foliage.

Crop rotation is a term that is most commonly used when growing edible plants. The principle is that some diseases (and pests) can be reduced if plants from the same family are not grown in the same place year after year. Crop rotation is particularly important with vegetables in the brassica family – such as broccoli, cabbage, kale and cauliflower – but it also extends to brassica-family members with fragrant flowers – such as night-scented stock, sweet rocket, stock, wallflowers and alyssum. If any diseases are noticed, it is best not to grow these plants or their brassica relatives in that same area for at least two years.

Despite our best efforts, diseases can still occur. Here are some products that can help control diseases in your fragrant garden.

This table is a general guide only. It's important to check product labels before spraying. Some products are not registered to control all diseases on all plants, particularly edible plants.

Ensure plants are not suffering from moisture stress when they're sprayed, because dehydrated plant foliage can be damaged. It's important to spray both sides of the leaves. Always use sprays as per the use and safety directions on the label.

DISEASE	SOLUTION
Black spot	Yates Rose Gun
Powdery mildew	Yates Rose Shield (Aust. only)
	Yates Super Shield (NZ only)
	Yates Nature's Way Fungus Spray (NZ only)
	Yates Mancozeb Plus Garden Fungicide & Miticide (Aust. only)
	Yates Fungus Fighter (NZ only)
Blight	Yates Mancozeb Plus Garden Fungicide & Miticide (Aust. only)
Botrytis (grey mould)	Yates Mancozeb Plus Garden Fungicide & Miticide (Aust. only)
	Remove and destroy infected foliage or flowers, reduce levels of humidity, don't water foliage, improve airflow.
Leaf spots	Yates Leaf Curl Copper Fungicide Spray (Aust. only)
	Yates Copper Oxychloride Fungicide (NZ only)
Downy mildew	Yates Liquid Copper Fungicide
	Yates Nature's Way Fungus Spray (NZ only)
	Yates Copper Oxychloride Fungicide (NZ only)
Root rot	Yates Anti Rot Phosacid Systemic Fungicide (Aust. only)
	Improve drainage and/or reduce watering.
Sooty mould	Control sap sucking insects with Yates Nature's Way Citrus & Ornamental Spray (Aust. only)
	Yates Nature's Way Organic Citrus, Vegie & Ornamental Spray (NZ only)
	Yates Rose Gun
Rust	Yates Rose Gun
	Yates Rose Shield (Aust. only)
	Yates Super Shield (NZ only)

TROUBLE-SHOOTING

Each of the 50 plant profiles in this book contains advice about the conditions that the plant likes, such as levels of light, watering and feeding. If a plant is not happy with the care it's receiving, or it's growing in a less-than-ideal spot, it will often exhibit symptoms that can provide clues about what might be amiss. Here are some of the most common symptoms and causes.

YELLOW LEAVES

- **Overwatering** – check moisture levels in the soil or potting mix with your finger and adjust watering according to the plant's needs. Some plants are particularly intolerant of a wet root zone.

- **Ageing leaves** – yellow leaves can be part of the natural process of ageing, before they fall from the plant. They can be trimmed off if desired.

- **Underfeeding** – pale foliage can indicate a lack of nutrients. Feed with a fast-acting complete liquid or soluble fertiliser. Also check the soil pH, because soil that is too alkaline or acidic can affect the availability of nutrients, leading to pale or discoloured plant foliage.

- **Too much sunlight** – plants that prefer a shadier spot can turn yellow or pale if subjected to too much light. Temporary shelter can be constructed; however, it's best to transplant the plants to a more protected location. Move potted plants to a shadier position.

- **Pests** – mite and aphid infestations can cause leaves to mottle and yellow. Check both sides of the leaves and along stems for signs of these pests.

- **Diseases** – check foliage for signs of diseases such as powdery mildew, which can often start with leaf yellowing.

- **Time to re-pot potted plants** – if a plant has been in the same pot for several years, it's likely that it has run out of space and nutrients. Re-pot into a slightly larger pot or refresh its existing potting mix.

TOP: Nutrient deficiency

BOTTOM: Yellowing caused by mites

BROWN LEAF TIPS

- **Overwatering** – check moisture levels in the soil or potting mix with your finger and adjust watering according to the plant's needs.

- **Sunburn** – harsh sun can sometimes singe leaf tips or, in severe cases, entire plants. Ensure sun-sensitive plants are grown in protected spots (shelter from the strong afternoon sun is particularly important) and plants are kept moist, particularly during hot dry weather. Potted sun-sensitive plants can be moved into a more protected location.

- **Overfeeding** – over-application of fertilisers can cause browning of leaf tips. Water the plant well (including potted plants) to help flush away excess nutrients, and reduce the amount and frequency of feeding.

WILTING

- **Underwatering** – leaves can wilt if the plant is not receiving enough water. Check moisture levels in the soil or potting mix with your finger and adjust watering according to the plant's needs.

- **Waterlogged soil** – poorly drained soil, potting mix or pots, or too much rainfall or watering, can lead to roots being starved of oxygen and roots rotting. Confusingly, the early symptom of excess water is drooping leaves. Check moisture levels in the soil or potting mix with your finger and adjust watering according to the plant's needs. In particular, plants that are intolerant of wet or poorly drained soil need to be planted in an area with better drainage (raised areas of well-drained soil can be created to improve the drainage) or grown in a pot that drains freely.

- **Root rot** – plants with root-rot disease will often start to wilt, due to their inability to absorb sufficient moisture. Check moisture levels in the soil or potting mix and adjust watering. In areas with heavy clay or poorly drained soil, grow plants in a raised mound of well-drained soil or in pots with good drainage. Apply a fungicide if required.

- **Cold damage** – warmth-loving plants can wilt when initially damaged by cold or frost, followed by the leaves burning, blackening or turning to mush. Grow plants in their preferred season and climate, make use of protected microclimates for sensitive plants, and cover vulnerable plants with frost cloth or apply an anti-transpirant spray such as Yates Waterwise DroughtShield.

SCORCHED LEAVES

- **Sunburn** – harsh sun, particularly if the plants are moisture stressed, can result in scorched leaves. Ensure moisture-loving plants are kept well-watered, particularly during hot dry weather. An anti-transpirant spray can help protect foliage. Move potted sun-sensitive plants into a more protected location.

LEGGY GROWTH

- **Insufficient sunlight** – sun-loving plants that are growing in shady spots can start to grow long and lanky stems as they search for light. Choose shade-tolerant plants for low-light areas, and move potted plants to a brightly lit spot.
- **Incorrect feeding** – too much nitrogen can sometimes lead to tall and spindly stems. Promote denser growth by feeding with a complete and balanced plant food.

LACK OF FLOWERS

- **Underfeeding** – flowering plants need higher levels of the nutrient potassium to promote flowering. Feed with a potassium-rich liquid plant food, such as Yates Thrive Rose & Flower Liquid Plant Food, which is specially formulated to encourage flowering.
- **Insufficient sunlight** – some plants need lots of sunshine to promote flowers. Grow plants in their preferred amount of sunlight, and move potted plants to a brightly lit spot to encourage flowering.

TOP: Root bound potted plant

BOTTOM: Sunburn

INDEX

Page numbers in **bold** indicate a plant's main entry; page numbers in *italics* indicate a photograph.

AUTHOR'S NOTE

Gardening is immensely good for you. Whether you're looking after a sprawling backyard or tending to a small collection of potted plants, gardening provides a connection to nature, and the process of caring for plants can be soul-soothing and great for improving your mental health.

I've always wanted to write about fragrant plants – they have a magical way of putting a smile on your face. Fragrance can be alluring and evocative, conjuring wonderful memories and emotions. Wandering around a garden, courtyard or balcony where you can enjoy not only gorgeous flowers but beautiful fragrance as well is uplifting. One of the best ways to enjoy fragrances is by growing the plants yourself. It's pure joy going into your garden throughout the year and inhaling the lovely aromas of perfumed flowers and foliage. So, the more scented plants you grow, the more colourful and grin-inducing your garden will be.

To my fabulous family, thank you for your support and patience while I wrote this book, and to Yates and the hardworking team at HarperCollins for your encouragement and willingness to bring this book idea to life.

PHOTOGRAPH CREDITS

ENDNOTES

1 news.rub.de/english/press-releases/2021-09-16-neurophysiologyhow-scents-take-meaning
2 seniorau.com.au/8586-smell-training-could-help-stopcognitive-decline
3 sharpbrains.com/blog/2019/03/18/study-finds-promise-in-smell-training-to-harness-neuroplasticity-and-improve-brain-health-in-older-adults/
4 pubmed.ncbi.nlm.nih.gov/19235739/
5 ncbi.nlm.nih.gov/pmc/articles/PMC5390566/

HarperCollins*Publishers*

Australia • Brazil • Canada • France • Germany • Holland • India
Italy • Japan • Mexico • New Zealand • Poland • Spain • Sweden
Switzerland • United Kingdom • United States of America

HarperCollins acknowledges the Traditional Custodians
of the land upon which we live and work, and pays respect
to Elders past and present.

First published in Australia in 2022
by HarperCollins*Publishers* Australia Pty Limited
Gadigal Country
Level 13, 201 Elizabeth Street, Sydney NSW 2000
ABN 36 009 913 517
harpercollins.com.au

A catalogue record for this book is available from the National Library of Australia

ISBN 978 1 4607 6267 7 (paperback)
ISBN 978 1 4607 1526 0 (ebook)

Cover and internal design by Jude Rowe, based on a design by Andy Warren
Front cover image © GAP Photos / Friedrich Strauss
Back cover image © David Burton–FLPA–Minden Pictures / AUSCAPE
Author photograph by Jacqueline Peck
Colour reproduction by Splitting Image Colour Studio, Clayton, Victoria
Printed and bound in China by RR Donnelley

8 7 6 5 4 3 2 1   22 23 24 25